Race To My Dream
Steven Wright

Front cover photos:
Racing pic by Nina Edminson Photography;
photo of Steve with Mister McGoldrick, courtesy of New Beginnings.
Back page photo:
Steve and Alexander.

Cover design and formatting by John Amy
www.ebookdesigner.co.uk

Contents

Steve and Alexander

Preface

This is the story of how, against all odds, my retired steeplechaser and I took on other horses and jockeys in a race.

Adelphi Warrior, known as Alexander, had not been on a racetrack for seven years. I was a hobby rider pushing sixty who had never raced before.

Taking part fulfilled a childhood dream – and was only possible because I became redundant and had the time to train for it.

Race To My Dream tells how we prepared for the race, and looks back at our seven-year rollercoaster ride of dramatic falls, uplifting triumphs and strange adventures that enabled us to take on our greatest challenge.

I began riding horses in my mid-forties as therapy for bankruptcy, a broken marriage and a drink problem but I never expected the racecourse to be my destination.

Along the way, Alexander and I fell for each other, hook, line and sinker, and that is why we were able to make my dream a reality. So I guess this is also a kind of love story.

I hope you enjoy our journey and share my pride in Alexander. Above all, if Race To My Dream leads to just one ex-racehorse getting a loving home and the chance of a happy new life, then this book will have been a success.

Chapter One

Race Day

The public address system crackled into life. I heard a voice boom out: "Good afternoon, ladies and gentlemen. Welcome to Skipton Races."

I had been to the local point-to-point steeplechase meeting before, but always as a spectator, never as a rider.

Soon the eyes of the crowd would be on me as I rode in my first ever horse race, at the age of fifty-eight. I perched on the edge of my seat in the sanctuary of the horse wagon and stared at the floor, alone with my thoughts. The air in the enclosed space of the living area was heavy with my nervous tension. My head felt thick with it. My stomach turned a somersault, as it had been doing all morning. I took a deep breath and slowly and deliberately exhaled, trying to clear my mind and slow down my heart rate.

Outside, my ex-racehorse, Alexander, let out a bellowing neigh of excitement. He had been unusually vocal since we arrived at the course. Soon, he and I would be galloping along the racetrack. My heart thumped at the thought. I took another deep breath.

I got to my feet and slowly fastened the buttons on my shiny racing silks and tucked them neatly into my white jockey breeches. Beneath my silks I wore a close-fitting sports vest and my body protector, a gift from an ex-jockey pal. It was old-fashioned and sturdy but I felt comfortable in it. I had rejected the offer of a pair of long racing boots because they were tight and pinched my calves. Instead, I wore my trusted short black boots. I had polished them that morning, rather than taking the breakfast my stomach would not allow me to eat. It was vital that everything I wore felt right for the huge challenge I was about to face. I would be galloping Alexander full pelt for one and a quarter miles against six rivals. I gazed critically at myself in the long mirror and wondered if it was a jockey staring back at me, or just a silly middle-aged dreamer? Perhaps I could be both.

There was a quiet knock on the door. A voice called out. "Are you decent?"

"Yes."

The door opened and the reassuring face of my friend Ian Conroy appeared. He and his wife Karen had looked after Alexander before and after his racing career. They had been indirectly responsible for bringing him into my life and few knew him better. Ian had not always seen eye to eye with my horse but he did not hesitate when I asked him to lead him up on race day.

"It will be an honour," he said, adding with a wry smile: "But I wish to emphasise, it will be a one off!"

"Don't worry," I replied. "It will be a one off for all of us!"

Now, Ian's strong and assured presence calmed my nerves.

"Are you ready?" he asked.

"Yes. I'm not wearing the racing boots. They don't feel comfortable."

"You do right, Steve. And there's no point putting on the goggles. The ground is good. The horses' hooves aren't going to be throwing up mud."

"And anyway," he added with a grin. "You need to be able to see where you're going!"

I smiled, despite the relentless churning of my tummy. I had yearned for this moment, but now it was here I was scared. The thought of us charging round the course while I desperately tried to avoid plummeting to the ground beneath the thundering hooves of the other horses suddenly terrified me.

The voice again echoed from the loudspeakers on the course: "So, we have seven runners and riders for the first race of the day, which is a charity race in aid of Candelighters."

Alexander responded with another huge neigh. I wondered how excited he was going to get.

Ian's expression became more serious. He looked at me and said: "It's time."

I picked up my jockey's skull cap, which was lined with thick protective padding and decked out in our bright yellow and purple racing colours. Attached to it was a head cam to record every moment of my big adventure – however it turned out! My outfit was completed by a pair of long, thin olive green riding socks emblazoned with the words Retraining of Racehorses. They were a prize from the charity when Alexander was the top ex-racehorse at a cross-country competition. It seemed appropriate to wear them. After all, I had retrained Alexander to do dressage and showjumping. Now I had trained him to race again.

I fastened my hat and stepped down from the wagon on to the lush grass. The air was resonant with the loud bleating of sheep calling to their lambs in the pasture next to the lorry park, but even this familiar sound of the spring countryside failed to sooth my jangling nerves. Now the moment had arrived, doubts pierced my mind like the thrusts of a dagger. Could I really do this? Did I even want to? Maybe it wasn't too late to back out. I wanted to scream: "No, let me out of here!"

And then I saw my horse. He was being held by Sue Dinsdale, my groom for the day. Sue rode Alexander regularly and, like me, had fallen in love with him. She had told her husband weeks ago not to make plans for this day. Alexander was tacked up and ready in his special lightweight racing saddle and orange rubber racing reins. He looked magnificent. He was tall, almost seventeen hands high, powerful and athletic. With his bright chestnut colouring and thin white blaze, he stood out. His ginger coat gleamed and shone like burnished copper. His muscles rippled and his smartly trimmed red mane and tail flowed in the light breeze.

"He looks really fit, Steve. You've done a fantastic job," Ian remarked.

I felt proud. We had worked hard to prepare for our race.

There was a glint in Alexander's eye and his ears were pricked as he took in his exciting new surroundings. I had been uncertain whether he would enjoy being back on the racecourse. There were no doubts now. He was obviously up for it and, as always, I took strength from him.

I strode up and patted his neck.

"Good lad," I said, and felt comforted.

My heart was still thumping but my mind was now clear. There was no going back. Of course I would ride in the race. I had been through too much to get here to quit now: bankruptcy, divorce, redundancy. Not to mention the trips to hospital after my terrible falls from Alexander in the early years. It had been a long, tough and often painful journey.

Sue led Alexander from the wagon park towards the parade ring. I marched resolutely alongside. I had watched other horses and riders make the same walk in the past. Now it was my horse being led up and I was the jockey who would be getting on.

Lost in my thoughts, I set off to my destiny.

I was bitten by the racing bug when I was a boy. Every Saturday afternoon I would eagerly tune into the horse racing on television. Watching those brave thoroughbreds leaping great steeplechase fences lifted my soul. I dreamed of riding in the Grand National.

I replicated my love of the sport through the racing board game, Totopoly, changing the names of the delicate plastic horses into those of real racehorses. Years later, when I played the game with my own children, I found old racehorse names, like Red Rum, Red Candle and Rouge Autumn, scribbled in blue ink in my childish handwriting on the inside of the battered box. By then, the horses were showing their age. Their fragile legs, and the heads of their jockeys, had been accidentally snapped off over the years. My favourite was a red horse, Leonidas II. Even with no front legs and a headless jockey, he still won for me. It never crossed my mind that one day I would own and ride a real red racehorse.

That day took decades to arrive. Meanwhile, my life took an altogether different course. It became a rollercoaster ride of debt and drink problems, marital breakdown and job insecurity. I nearly fell off the ride more than once, but with grit and determination I stuck on. I found it equally hard to stay on board when I finally got my racehorse. By then I was in my fifties and believed my racing dream had long passed me by.

But it was only just beginning.

My musing was interrupted by the braying of the public address system.

"The horses for the first race are now in the parade ring."

I looked around and took in my surroundings. Behind the grassed paddock was a large white pavilion that housed the jockeys' changing rooms, the weighing-in area and the race officials' tent. Beyond the ring, I could see rows of bookmakers, their electronic boards lit up in red. To the side were the beer tent, stalls and food vans. On the far side of the line of bookmakers, enthusiastically shouting out their odds, I glimpsed the racetrack. It went round a long bend in front of us and disappeared down the far side of the course and up a steep hill. At the top, it turned left again and came down the other side of the hill to the finish. The winning post was at the end of the final straight. Soon I would be galloping my horse along that track in front of a crowd of race fans. And what a crowd it was. There were hundreds of people gathering on both sides of the track and around the Winners Enclosure. It was a Bank Holiday Saturday at the end of April and the racing was a popular attraction. In the distance, I could see lines of vehicles coming through the entrance gates and being parked up on the field.

I watched in awe and disbelief as Alexander marched purposefully around the parade ring. It was something I thought I would never see. But now the truth hit home. He was a racehorse once more. And I was his jockey.

Spectators gathered to look at Alexander and the other six runners in the race. I had expected him to be nervous and jumpy, to prance about and tug Sue's arms out, but he was very chilled.

"He looks so relaxed," I said to Ian.

"He'll be a different horse when he gets out on the course," Ian grinned back.

That was my worry, that I would not be able to handle him with his 'racehorse head' on. I would soon find out.

It was seven years since Alexander had last raced. He was well bred and his pedigree suggested he should have done well but his steeplechasing career had been brief and unspectacular. At just six years old, he had been thrown on the scrapheap. Now, aged thirteen, he was about to run his first Flat race.

I gazed about me, wondering what I should do while I waited to get on. The whole situation seemed unreal. I noticed that some of the bookies' boards were lit up with the names of horses and their odds. I didn't think they would be taking bets on a charity race, but clearly they were. Glancing across at one of the boards, I swore out loud in amazement.

"We're the bloody favourites!"

The bookie had Alexander at 6-4 to win the race.

"That's ridiculous! No pressure, then," I exclaimed. It seemed that friends from our livery yard had all put money on us, bringing our odds in. Other punters had seen the move and thought we were a good thing.

A pal grinned and shouted to the bookie: "I think you're on to a winner there, mate! The jockey's fifty-eight and the horse has only been in training for three weeks!"

The time for the off was drawing nearer. I was still nervous, but I was also determined. I was starting to focus on the race and how I was going to ride it. I was there to try and win. For the one and only time in my life I could pit my wits against other jockeys in the hurly burly of a race. It was what I had always wanted to do. Now I had to get on and do it. I looked across at Alexander, but this time I felt excitement, an anticipation of the thrill of the race. I wanted to leap on this wonderful horse, who I so loved and admired, and start to gallop him. As I walked purposefully into the parade ring, I heard a woman call out: "Good luck, Mr Steve!" I glanced up to see a friend from the yard, smiling and waving. She had witnessed my darkest riding day, four years earlier, when I was badly injured in a horrible accident. Now she had taken time off work in the hope of sharing in my most glorious day. In the next fifteen minutes I would know whether it was to be glory or bitter disappointment.

The public address system burst back into life.

"Jockeys mount please," it instructed. And then it repeated, so there was no doubt: "Jockeys mount please."

This was it.

Ian and Sue had halted Alexander in the middle of the parade ring. It was time for me to get on. I was dreading this moment. All jockeys get the leg up, but I wasn't used to it and feared I would make a fool of myself in front of our friends and the growing audience.

Ian had done little to reassure me.

"The first time I got legged up, I flew over the horse and landed on the floor on the other side!" he told me.

Another rider was using a mounting block to get on her horse in the usual way. I thought about following suit. As I hovered indecisively, Ian called out: "Come on Steve, I'll give you a leg up."

The decision had been made for me. I tried to look casual as I bent my left leg and Ian took hold of it.

"Bounce with your other leg," he instructed. "One, two, three," and then he hoisted me up. I tried to swing my right leg over Alexander's back, but it fell short. My worst fears were realised. While everybody watched, I was left half on and half off my horse, puffing and straining to get into place. For a moment I thought I would slide off the side of him. But Ian kept shoving and after shuffling about like a stranded beetle for a second or two, I flopped into the saddle. It was neither elegant nor professional, but I was on board. I slipped my right foot into the stirrup but added to my embarrassment by nervously fiddling about with my left foot for several seconds before finally thrusting it in place. At last I was in position.

With a "Good luck, Steve," Sue left Ian in charge of the reins. Her words were echoed by a voice somewhere in the crowd.

Now my focus was on Alexander. He was edgy. He knew

the race was near and he was getting psyched up for it. He threw his head around, but Ian had a strong hold on the bridle.

"Give him a bit more rein, Steve," he advised. "The more you relax, the more he will."

I slipped the reins a couple of inches, aware only of my horse and Ian at our side. I was glad he was there. He kept giving me advice and I took it all in, grunting short replies.

"Just remember, when you start cantering down to post, he'll be quite strong with you."

Then Ian chuckled: "He's certainly come alive now, hasn't he?"

Alexander was still tossing his head, keen to start running. We were one of the last to leave the paddock and begin heading down the grassed walkway towards the course.

"Give him a pat," Ian encouraged. "Let me know when you're happy and I'll let you go."

I took one final deep breath and looked ahead at the racecourse, now stretching away right in front of us. "Yeah, all right."

"Okay?"

"Yeah."

"Right. Enjoy yourself."

And with that, Ian let go of the reins.

Ian Conroy leads us out to the course
(Picture: Nina Edminson Photography)

Chapter Two

A Big Gamble

Six months earlier, riding in a race was the last thing on my mind. With my sixtieth birthday just over the horizon, I faced a major crossroads in my life. After forty years working as a journalist, I was suddenly given the option of bringing down the curtain on an exciting and successful career. The Bradford Telegraph & Argus, where I had been the crime reporter for thirteen years, offered me voluntary redundancy. It was a golden opportunity to take the money and run – and probably the only one I would get. But I knew it was a gamble. If I accepted, what would I do next, and how would I pay for everything when there was no money left? It was a question I had asked myself before.

I was born and bred in Leeds. In my mid-teens, I made up my mind to be a journalist. In 1977, the Sheffield Star, an evening paper of some repute, advertised for two trainee reporters. A couple of hundred would-be newshounds applied. The weeks dragged by. I was anxious to know my fate. The deputy editor told me later that, after the umpteenth call from me to ask if they had made up their minds, he declared: "That Steve Wright is making my life hell. Sign him up!" And so began almost a decade of provincial daily news reporting. I was then offered a job back in West Yorkshire as a freelance journalist with a national news agency.

I married in 1991 and had three children, Emma, Sophie and Ben, but as the years went by, the marriage disintegrated. The end of the relationship was hastened by my ever growing financial difficulties. Like my drinking, they spiralled out of control.

I have always liked a drink. I was about seventeen when I started downing pints of Tetley's bitter or mild, washed down with a few Southern Comforts, at my local pub, the Brown Cow. Though I drank more than was good for me, I was never an alcoholic. But by the late 1990s, as my life became more miserable and chaotic, the drink became an escape.

Drinking was part of a journalist's job. If you wanted to get the best stories, you had to go to the pub and talk to people. I did that regularly for years. Then, when things got tough, I turned to alcohol.

The news agency had made good money rolling out the exclusives during the Yorkshire Ripper inquiry. But by the 1990s, the bubble had burst. As the new millennium dawned, the boss of the agency decided to retire and offered to sell the business to me. The price was high and I didn't even have the money for a cheap holiday. I was in serious debt. Loans and credit cards were piling up and any spare money I had was going on the booze. To buy the business I needed a £20,000 bank loan, if I could find the cash to match it. The only way I could do that was to ask my parents to dig into their savings. They were uncomfortable about the deal. They sensed, rightly, that something didn't add up but they could see how much I wanted it, so they supported me with hard cash. I let my heart overrule my head and did the deal. It was the biggest mistake of my life, costing me my marriage, my home and my car, not to mention my happiness and almost my sanity.

The deal was to pay most of the purchase price up front and

the rest in monthly instalments over three years. It didn't take long to realise that the burden of those payments, allied to wages for two members of staff, office rent and tax demands, far outweighed what I was earning. It didn't help that I was having to spend half my time chasing money I was owed, and often not getting it. I was forced to sell our neat little semi-detached house. It was nothing special but it was our home, which we had worked hard for, and it hurt to leave. I gave up the office and rented a large detached bungalow, big enough to combine home and work. But the rent matched the size of the property.

I knew the end was near the day a burly man came to the front door to repossess my shiny blue Citroen Xsara estate car because I was so far behind with the repayments. I felt a terrible emptiness and a sense of total failure as I watched it disappear out of sight down the road.

By December 2002, feeling crushed, I was forced to endure the embarrassment of going to Bradford County Court to declare myself bankrupt. It was a humiliating low point in my life.

I had worked in Bradford for thirty years, first for the agency and, from 2003, for the Telegraph and Argus. Bradford is a wonderful place to be a journalist. There is always something happening there. But after three decades, the novelty was wearing thin. In my late fifties I was getting tired of the daily grind, and beginning to feel overpowered by the unpleasant, nasty and pure evil individuals I had to write about.

There wasn't much I hadn't seen in that time, but the day a member of the public hurled a missile at a crown court judge as he passed sentence was a first. The half-full plastic water bottle whizzed across the packed courtroom, thumped into the wall behind him and clattered to the floor. Lawyers, probation officers and reporters turned in disbelief towards the public seating area where a scruffily dressed young woman was on her feet. Her plain features contorted with anger, she stretched out an arm and pointed an accusing finger at the judge.

"You fucking old bastard!" she shouted.

The judge adjusted his wig, peered over the little lenses of his spectacles and fixed her with a steely stare as she continued to shout abuse.

He spoke quietly but firmly: "Have that woman arrested."

Friends tried to quieten her and pull her back into her seat. But still she stood and swore. Others in the public seating area joined in the pandemonium, rising to their feet and adding their voices to the abuse.

"Will everybody sit down and be quiet," the court clerk pleaded, and was ignored.

Three burly security officers, summoned by the clerk, marched into the court. Two of them grabbed the woman by the arms and began to remove her. But she was not going to go quietly.

"Get off me, you bastards!" she yelled, and flailed wildly at the guards.

But they were too strong and hoisted her out through the doors. Her voice could still be heard, less piercing now but just as strident.

A ferret-faced young woman scuttled after her, calling out her support.

And then the court resumed its dignity.

The judge sighed, long and regretfully. He was an experienced member of the judiciary, based at Bradford Crown Court, and he understood the local communities. He knew what made the criminals and their victims tick. I had known him for many years, since he was a barrister. He was a fair and compassionate man, the last person to deserve such abuse.

Now he resumed his sentencing duties. Addressing the young woman in the dock, he spoke ruefully. "As I was about to explain, that sentence of imprisonment will be suspended for two years. That means if you commit no further offences in that time, and you carry out unpaid work for the community, you will hear no more of this. You are free to go."

The woman had played a minor part in a horrific incident of violent disorder in Bradford city centre. Her role had been fleeting, and it was obvious from the judge's remarks that he was going to give her a suspended sentence. But her friend in the public gallery had been too emotional to see that. She spent a night in the cells for her outburst while the defendant she thought had been wronged walked free. The woman protester was unrepentant the next day. But the judge, merciful as ever, released her with a warning.

Others in the dock were given long prison sentences for their roles in the disturbance. It had been a particularly unpleasant case. CCTV footage was played to the court that showed truly sickening violence. The images of people being beaten, stamped on, hit with bottles and mercilessly kicked in the head and body while helpless on the ground shocked even hardened detectives and journalists like myself. The throwing of the bottle at the judge topped it all off. It was one of those days when you lose faith in humanity. When the evil, brutal and moronic behaviour of some human beings takes away all pleasure and hope. It is a feeling that starts to get all too common when you have worked in Bradford for so long and seen it at first hand so many times.

Driving home from work that night, I felt very down. The evening commute, always dreary and frustrating, seemed more miserable than ever. I was in an endless queue of vehicles inching forward through the grim, depressing city. Stop start, bumper to bumper, we crawled along. Scruffy grey buildings slipped slowly by. We were overtaken on foot by a down and out, trudging dirtily along and shouting to himself and the world. My despair seemed complete. Home was miles away, and felt further.

On Manningham Lane - a main thoroughfare leading from the city centre, through inner city decay and eventually to freedom - the monotony was suddenly broken by the loud revving of an engine behind us. I glanced in my wing mirror and saw a powerful 'boy racer' car zooming up on the wrong side of the carriageway. It swept past. Oncoming motorists were forced to slow down as the white Subaru sped towards them. Then the driver, a young Asian man, suddenly slammed on his brakes and screeched off down a side street towards the Bradford City football ground. It was a reckless and idiotic piece of driving, but not unusual. The city is plagued by selfish and inconsiderate hotheads behind the wheel, without a thought for anyone else on the roads or pavements. You drive at your peril in Bradford.

The start of the working week was the worst time, that 'here we go again' feeling that overwhelmed me on a Monday morning. And the pressure was on from the moment I walked into the office.

The newspaper industry is slowly dying, nibbled at persistently by the digital age and the availability of news in so many media forms. Papers like the Telegraph & Argus had to change, and that change did not sit easily with older, traditional journalists like myself. I joked about being the office dinosaur and struggled to get my head round the ever-evolving digital technology, feeling that my old fashioned skills as a reporter were becoming less needed. I was starting to feel very out of place.

As the American owned company relentlessly cut staff, the remaining reporters were left with their backs firmly to the wall. There were more than twenty reporters when I joined the Telegraph & Argus. That figure had more than halved. I often wondered how we managed to get a paper out at all.

The noose seemed to be drawing ever tighter. The last round of redundancies had involved our four photographers, who were left to fight it out for one job that combined taking photos with running the picture desk. I asked myself how a newspaper could operate without photographers. It didn't take long to get the answer. The reporters would have to take many of the photos and upload them on to the Telegraph & Argus website. And if a newspaper could make its photographers redundant, I reckoned it could get rid of anybody – including me. Christmas was often a time when the company made grim staffing announcements. I always feared the next festive season would be my last.

The pressure was constant. Each day began with early demands for 'filler copy,' otherwise known as news in brief, followed by the morning meeting with the news desk when you were expected to come up with a long list of stories for the next day's paper. At the end of the shift, I was physically and mentally worn out.

What kept me going through the long days was the camaraderie with my colleagues, a great bunch of people. There weren't many of us left, but we smiled at adversity and made jokes about our plight. It was the only way to survive.

"We need lots of stories today. Everything has been used up at the weekend. Get your thinking caps on," barked the news editor.

My mate, Rhys Thomas, sitting opposite me, glanced across and I raised my eyebrows at him.

"No time to look at my great jumping photos from yesterday, then," I said ruefully.

My colleagues weren't horsey but they always showed an

interest in my equine adventures.

"Not more pictures of some silly old buffer hitting the deck," Rhys replied with a grin.

He was never short of a joke at my expense, and I liked him all the better for it. I smiled back and got on with my work. But everything was about to change.

For several years I had watched colleagues being made redundant. Some, particularly those with young families to support, were left distraught. Others seemed happy to take the money offered and then walk back through the door a few weeks or months later to do their old jobs on a freelance basis. I envied them.

I had twice asked about the possibility of voluntary redundancy, and twice been told it was out of the question. I resigned myself to the possibility that the only redundancy I might get would be forced on me.

But one morning in October 2016, the news editor took me to one side.

"Are you still interested in voluntary redundancy?" he asked.

There were rumours of more changes on the way that would make our working conditions even more demanding and unpleasant. And the hell of Christmas was now approaching. For years, Christmas had been spoiled by the crazy demands for extra stories in the weeks before it, to fill seasonal editions of the paper that most people were not going to buy anyway.

Not so much old news, as unread news.

The pressure on the reporters was enormous and sucked every drop of comfort and joy out of them.

And the company didn't even bother to give us a festive bottle of wine in return. That small but welcome gift, wheeled round the old Dickensian newsroom on the third floor, had long disappeared.

Days later I met the editor. A redundancy offer soon followed, bringing my thirteen years of employment at the Telegraph & Argus to an abrupt end. I felt desperately sorry for the workmates I was leaving behind. It could only get harder for them.

But I had no regrets as I walked out of the back door for the last time. Almost immediately, a great weight seemed to lift from my shoulders. I knew I was taking a huge gamble on getting another job at my age. But I was certain it was the right decision.

My redundancy money would last six to eight months and for the moment I was happy to sit back and enjoy my new found freedom.

The pure pleasure of riding my horse over the hills near our livery yard whenever I pleased can perhaps only be fully appreciated by someone who casts off the shackles as recklessly as I did!

Chapter Three

In Denial

I had owned Alexander for almost seven years and throughout that time the idea of racing him had tantalised me. Most people thought I was barmy to even consider it. After all, I was a middle-aged hobby rider, not a jockey. One who had suffered numerous dramatic and painful falls from my ex-racehorse. My track record was not encouraging.

I have always loved horses but I did not ride regularly until I was in my mid-forties. My childhood was non-equestrian except for a couple of sedate pony treks while on holiday with my parents. I was unaware of any history of horse riding in the family until I discovered that my grandad had served in the cavalry during the First World War and ridden in point-to-point races. In my thirties, I spent a few months plodding round at a riding school but although I loved those Saturday morning rides, I learned precious few equestrian skills.

All that changed when I met my partner Jenny. I got to know her at Leeds Crown Court. She was covering cases for the Telegraph & Argus, while I went there to report on the big murder trials. There was a bitter rivalry between us for the front page stories. We saw one another regularly in the crown court press room but attraction was far from instantaneous on either side. All I saw was a stressy rival wanting to take my stories. I was a smoker in those days and sat in the press room, wreathed in blue vapour, dourly phoning my copy to the office before joining other male hacks for a few pints. Jenny thought I was arrogant and rather seedy.

Back in more generous times, the newspaper group held a lavish Christmas party, treating the staff to a splendid buffet, free drinks and a live band. In December 2004, the bash was held at Valley Parade, the football stadium rebuilt after the Bradford City Fire Disaster. Jenny, who had been persuaded at the last minute to attend, arrived on a coach from Skipton with journalists from the local weekly paper. They sat round a large circular table, having a good time. Jenny looked happy and was laughing a lot. I was struck by how attractive she was. She had a bewitching smile and her eyes danced and sparkled. I went to the bar and as I returned with my drink, I stopped to talk to her. It was probably the first time I had been nice to her.

I returned to the Telegraph & Argus table. After a few minutes, my colleagues got up to dance, but I stayed where I was. Soon afterwards, Jenny came to join me. We began chatting and it seemed like we had been friends for years. We soon found we had something in common, a love of horses. She owned three and told me all about her black Irish mare and her latest acquisitions, a young gipsy trotter called Daniel and his half-brother, a yearling known as Baby Horse.

I began riding Jenny's two older horses but my early outings were marked by a worrying lack of control. I first rode the black mare but she was big and powerful and took off with me on an unplanned gallop along a puddled track. Great splashes of water and clods of mud were hurled in the air by her flying hooves as we thundered along. The dark greatcoat I rather oddly wore, giving me the Cossack look, flapped wildly in the sheer momentum of the mare's magnificently untamed approach. Jenny likened the vision of the flying black horse and the cloaked, hunched, dark figure to the Devil Rides Out.

The dramas continued when I rode Daniel. There was something special about my first encounter with him. When I looked into his stable my gaze was met by a pair of deep, black unblinking eyes, searching out my very soul. I could see wariness in them, and anger, and a great intelligence. But there was something else. An instant strange trust and affection.

Daniel had a big chip on his shoulder. He had been tethered near the motorway in Bradford and his new life on a smart livery yard had left him strangely resentful, like an urchin sent to a posh boarding school. At the merest hint of any slight, his coarse, bog brush mane bristled with indignation and his boot-button eyes glared with a smouldering fury. But his huge personality soon captured my heart.

Daniel lived for mealtimes, devouring his food with voracious concentration, but when it came to riding him, he needed plenty of persuasion to do anything at all. The only time he showed any real enthusiasm was when it came to getting rid of his rider, with his sudden 'spin and go' technique. I can't remember the first fall I had from Daniel, and I quickly lost count. It became commonplace to see him disappearing into the distance with his reins and stirrups flapping, while I angrily puffed after him, shouting: "Come back here, you little git!"

We were practicing in the showjumping field one evening when Daniel noticed we had an audience. Just yards away, half a dozen calves were peering at him over a stone wall. Daniel was horrified. In his alarm, he took a huge leap over the jump, turned sharp left and ran in the opposite direction to escape. It was too much for my flimsy riding skills.

Daniel's biggest fear was of birds flying out of the undergrowth. The pheasant season was never a good time to take him into the fields. A bird would suddenly emerge, flapping wildly and calling raucously, and fly past his nose. Just as suddenly, Daniel would perform his spin and go act. The result was always the same.

I was determined to stay in the saddle if I could and I learned to cling on grimly when he pitched me up round his neck. I once ended up with my legs flailing and my arms wrapped round him as if in a lover's embrace. He carried on cantering and I found myself sliding under him until I was gazing up into his eyes. Whatever my expression, it was not one of love at that moment. Somehow, I clambered back into the saddle and pulled him up.

The combination of a young horse, nervous about jumping, and a rookie rider, who was weak in the leg and loose in the saddle, made for great entertainment when Daniel and I began taking part in local shows. I decided to call him In Denial when we competed. It was an anagram of his name, and also suited his stubborn streak. You could almost hear him saying, when he refused yet another fence: "I deny I want to jump that."

Daniel and I earned our first showjumping rosette in dramatic fashion in a Pairs competition. Our partners had jumped a fast clear round. Then it was our turn. Daniel warily pottered towards the first fence. Two strides out he dug in his toes and stopped. I swung him round, gave him a couple of hearty kicks and he hopped reluctantly over. Daniel always had a high opinion of himself, and realising he had an audience, he began to warm to his task. We got over the next four fences at a brisk trot, then turned across the centre of the arena towards the sixth fence, stripy with a spread and looking extremely large to me. Clearly it was just as unattractive to Daniel, who whipped away in consternation. I turned him in again, kicked like mad and shouted: "Come on, Dan!" Terrified, he ballooned the jump and I found myself clinging round his neck in desperation. The spectators gasped, expecting me to hit the ground at any moment. Defying gravity, I shuffled myself back into the saddle as Daniel trundled on. Cue more gasps from the watchers, who were getting their best entertainment of the day. Still completely unbalanced, I booted Daniel into the next obstacle. To his credit, he hopped over and, picking up on the excitement and enthusiastic encouragement of the crowd, he burst into a canter to hurdle the last couple of fences. We surged through the finish to cheers and applause.

It would not be the last time we would get sympathetic support for being the unorthodox underdogs.

My haphazard riding wasn't the only thing that made me look a complete fool in the company of skilled local equestrians. I am not very practical and the tack, especially the seemingly endless pieces of the bridle, was a mystery to me. Left to my own devices in the stable, I could create mayhem and confusion. I was once caught trying to work out what had gone wrong when I put the saddle on back to front. I also unwittingly devised a quick and efficient way to untack Daniel, mistakenly undoing the bridle cheekpieces, allowing the bit to fall to the floor and the whole thing to easily unhook from his ears.

Tying up haynets proved equally troublesome. I would knot them up so ineptly that they had to be cut down. There was also the ridiculous incident when I knocked myself out on Daniel's saddle rack. I was skipping him out when I banged my head hard on the shiny red metal frame, and being bald the impact was all the greater. I was knocked out cold and lay unconscious in the straw at the back of the stable until I woke to see Daniel peering down at me, his boot-button eyes glowing with what I felt sure was amusement. No one had bothered to come to look for me because I was very slow at skipping out. I always spent so long poking about delicately in the straw with one fork prong that I had not been missed.

I worked hard on my riding and began to improve, though it was slow progress. I watched more competent riders and tried to copy them, shortening my 'washing line' reins. I was complemented on my soft hands and balance, and began to form an effective partnership with Daniel and to fall off him less often.

But my weak seat and flapping lower leg remained a problem for years, and when Alexander arrived, it didn't take long to find out how much better I needed to become.

Chapter Four

The Dream Chaser

Alexander was born on a farm in Kendal, Cumbria, on March 23, 2004. His mother was a retired racehorse called Gun Shot, who won three hurdle races. She was feisty and has been described to me by people who knew her as 'psycho' and 'evil.' Alexander inherited her bright chestnut colouring but, fortunately, few of her personality disorders!

His dad was Alflora, a moderately successful Flat horse who finished sixth in the 1992 Epsom Derby. But it was at stud that Alflora earned his real fame, becoming Britain's leading sire of steeplechasers on five occasions. He died in 2016 at the ripe old age of 27.

I was lucky enough to meet him a few years earlier, at the Shade Oak Stud in Shropshire, where he spent most of his life. Alflora was in the steam room when I first set eyes on him, and he left a lasting impression. Here was this tall, muscular dark bay horse, gleaming and steaming, and proud. He looked every inch a star. I watched in awe as he was put on the indoor horse walker, where he marched round purposefully at the front. This was a real athlete. Then came the highlight of my visit. Most stallions are sharp and lively and need special handling, so I wasn't expecting to get close to Alflora, but he was a very laid back horse and I was offered his lead rope. And there I was, standing proudly at the head of Alexander's famous dad. As

Alflora was a grandson of the Derby winner, Nijinsky, Alexander is a great-grandson of one of the greatest ever racehorses.

Alexander was christened 'Alfie' after his father, and was the eldest of Gun Shot's three foals. She sadly died after giving birth for the third time. When he was less than eight months old, Alexander was taken to the Tattersalls sales in Ireland, but he did not reach the 9,500 Euros asking price and returned to the farm in Kendal. He was first ridden when he was aged two or three by former professional jump jockey Brian Storey, who described him as a lovely, laid back horse, who 'looked the part.'

Alexander stayed at the farm for the next couple of years and when he was four he again went to the sales, this time at Doncaster, but was withdrawn from the auction. He was then sold to Ian and Karen Conroy, and without their kindness and patience his life could have taken an altogether different path. Ian recalls 'a fat chestnut horse with a big belly,' and soon renamed him 'Herman Monster' because he had an attitude problem.

"He didn't want to do anything. He wouldn't even leave the yard. He would rear and go into reverse. He went backward faster than he went forward and he would sit down while you were on him," Ian told me.

"He was very cunning when he didn't want to do something and would reverse quickly towards the nearest parked car."

It was Karen who persuaded Alexander to leave the confines of the yard.

"I kept riding him to the gate and then turning him away from it. He was very puzzled. He began thinking: 'Why don't we just go through it?' I had no trouble with him after that."

Ian and Karen bred and raised horses for the racing world and they were contacted by a businessman who wanted to own a racehorse.

Trainer Martin Todhunter, who runs a professional jumps yard in Cumbria, came to look at Alexander, liked what he saw and took him on. But his stay at the Todhunter yard was brief. He took a dislike to the mechanical horse walker, refusing to move and bringing it to a halt. Raceyard staff were forced to chase him round and get him off it.

Alexander was moved to a point-to-point yard in Durham to be trained for amateur steeplechasing the following year, when he would be six years old. He made his debut, under the racing name Adelphi Warrior, in a three-mile Open Maiden race, for horses that haven't won, on February 7, 2010, at Witton Castle in Durham. There were seven runners and Alexander was a 5-1 chance in the betting. He trailed in last of the six finishers, a considerable distance behind the winner. His jockey reported he had jumped well but he hadn't been quick enough between his fences.

His second run, a month later at Dalston, Cumbria, was also an Open Maiden race. This time there were 15 runners and he was well fancied, at 4-1. But though he again jumped well, he got behind and his jockey pulled him up.

And that was the end of Alexander's racing career. Though he was still physically and mentally immature, as far as his businessman owner was concerned he had already failed and the deal was off. It was fortunate for Alexander that he was returned to Ian and Karen. Not every unsuccessful racehorse is so lucky. But the couple have caring hearts and they wanted him to have a secure future after racing.

Within weeks, the handsome chestnut gelding had caught the eye of Mark Grunnill, a friend of Ian and Karen who lived a couple of miles away. But not long after Mark bought him, Alexander threw him off, landing him in hospital with a painful leg injury. Mark and his partner, Alison Oliver, decided they had to sell Alexander. The unpredictable thoroughbred was now facing a very uncertain future.

But our paths were about to cross. Destiny was just around the corner.

At about the same time Alexander was running his second and final race, I had the thrill and privilege of meeting Yorkshire racing legend, Mister McGoldrick. The steeplechaser was my favourite racehorse. He was trained by Sue Smith and her husband, former showjumping star Harvey Smith, at their stables high on Bingley Moor, not far from Bradford. Although I had enjoyed days at race meetings at Wetherby and Haydock, I had never been close up to a racehorse. It was my job as a journalist that gave me the opportunity to meet Mister McGoldrick when I persuaded our features editor to run a magazine article on him.

Mister McGoldrick won fifteen races, earned more than £370,000 in prize money, and provided the trainer with her first winner at the Cheltenham Festival, the blue riband of jumps racing. He was thirteen years old and a racing veteran when I met him, but his enthusiasm was undimmed and retirement was not yet an option. I had always loved his front-running style; bold, spectacular jumping; and unquenchable will to win. I turned up at the Smith stables on a cold and drizzly morning, but my heart was warmed when I was allowed to hold Mister McGoldrick on a lead rope, and feed him a mint. It was a dream come true and all the inspiration I needed to get my own racehorse.

Two months later, I had him.

Like Alexander, my equestrian future was unclear. I wanted to compete successfully at local cross-country events and to do that I needed a fast, enthusiastic horse who could jump. Neither Daniel nor his younger brother, Baby Horse, were suitable.

After much heart-searching, we decided that Baby would be happier with a quieter life. We advertised him for sale in the hope that I would then find my perfect horse. Less than two weeks after the advert first appeared, Mark and Alison came to see Baby. Alison rode him down the leafy lane from our livery stables and said she felt safe and secure as Baby trundled contentedly along. She wanted a quiet horse to ride out from their rural home on the estuary near Grange-over-Sands in Cumbria. Baby would hack out along the sea wall, through nearby woodland and down flat country lanes. It sounded ideal.

The couple took Baby on a month-long trial with a view to buy. We arranged to visit him at his new home a couple of days later.

"What sort of horse are you looking for to replace Baby?" asked Mark, just before the couple set off back to Cumbria.

"We're not in any hurry," Jenny replied. "We'll probably wait until next year and then look for something that Steve can do cross-country on. Something safe and experienced."

Mark looked thoughtful. Then he announced that he had just what we were after. A young 16.3hh ex-racehorse called Herman. The one that had landed him in hospital.

Jenny was horrified. She politely told Mark that was the last sort of horse we would ever want. But she failed to see the glint of excitement in my eye!

Mark and Alison's home was reached down a winding rural lane over a picturesque wooden bridge. The house was bounded by lush fields, where black and white cattle munched peacefully and calves and lambs frolicked. Plump hens and a noisy cockerel roamed freely on the big lawn and a friendly dog basked in the sunshine. Across the rich pastureland could be glimpsed the estuary with its cruel but wonderful tides.

Mark was still limping from his nasty fall when he greeted us. Alison took us straight to where Baby was grazing with a pony in a paddock beside the house. He ambled over, permitted us to pat him for a couple of minutes, then wandered off with his new friend. Clearly, he was a contented horse.

We sat at a wooden table overlooking the fields and the distant estuary. The hens strutted confidently round our feet as Alison served coffee and an array of homemade cakes. The dog joined in the hopeful scavenging for titbits.

It was a lovely, relaxing afternoon, but for Jenny there was a rather large cloud on the horizon. Nothing had so far been said, but at the far side of the paddock was something tall, in a glinting gold fly rug and matching hat, and with a long, drooping pelican-like head. It seemed quite happy to stand bathing in the spring sunshine and Jenny fervently hoped it would stay where it was.

I, too, had spotted it. It was indeed tall. It was also lean and athletic, and orange in colour. It looked wonderful to me. I prayed that our hosts were not going to forget about it. The minutes passed but as the afternoon drew to a close, Mark fetched a lead rope and brought Herman to the gate.

I was transfixed. I had never seen anything quite like him close up. The nearer you got to him, the taller he seemed to get. He had big, powerful shoulders and a muscular back end. There wasn't an ounce of fat on him. He was almost skinny. His big, light brown eyes rolled uncertainly, and rather disconcertingly, but he seemed meek enough. Not the sort of chap, on the face of it, you would expect to put you in hospital.

Mark went to the house to fetch the tack while I got my riding hat from the car. Herman was obedient as the bridle was put on. The saddle fitted cosily over a big, furry brown pad, giving him the appearance of a drum major's horse.

Herman was led out of the garden and made to stand just outside the gates on the edge of the lane. I was wondering how to get on this tall orange creature, when an old wooden stool was produced to be used as a mounting block. Jenny could only stand back and watch in dismay as I prepared to sit on my first racehorse.

My heart was in my mouth as I tottered nervously on the stool. As I pushed up to swing my leg across Herman's back, I accidentally kicked the stool backwards and it toppled to the ground with a clatter. I caught my breath, expecting the horse to react in some ridiculously athletic way that would leave me on the floor in great pain. But Mark had a strong hold on him. There was a little twitch from the thoroughbred, and then nothing. Herman was standing perfectly still, with me sitting on top of him. It was an odd feeling, unreal and yet right.

"Okay?" asked Mark.

"Fine," I replied, more nonchalantly than I felt.

Mark led us into the lane. Hardly anyone lived down this pretty backwater so the chance of meeting any traffic was remote. That was a blessing.

"Are you all right to take charge?" said Mark, knowing the answer and letting the reins go.

And then we were off on our first ride together. I had never sat on a thoroughbred, let alone one that had been racing just a few weeks before. I didn't know what to expect.

We set off down the road at a brisk walk.

"Bloody hell," I thought.

Even at that pace, the difference from the horses I had ridden before was astonishing. Herman bounced, and sprang, and swayed. He was alive with movement. Each step he took moved me around in the saddle in a way that was disconcerting and yet exhilarating. He had an incredible rhythm and I was surprised to find that I was quickly able to move with it and get in time with him.

Then we trotted for the first time. I thought Herman might take off with me because we were going faster. But he didn't.

He just trotted in that same lovely rhythm and I joined in with the music. It was magical and I could have carried on all afternoon.

There was no escape after that. I had to own him.

I dismounted and Herman was led away to be untacked. He then ambled off to graze in his paddock. He had taken it all in his long stride, almost robotically. But he was a robot with great style.

Fearing my mind was made up, Jenny whispered: "I don't like its head, it's all long and thin."

"All racehorse heads are like that," I hissed back, offended.

Already, I felt a protective bond towards this wonderful, if totally alien, orange creature.

We sat down to reflect over another coffee. Mark fetched Herman's passport and I reverently studied the fascinating booklet. Encased in a smart, racing green-coloured binder, it was stamped by the British Horseracing Authority and stated his parentage was DNA tested and approved.

This was the racehorse I had dreamed of owning. Now, clutching his passport, the opportunity was literally within my grasp. Jenny remained unconvinced but she accepted the inevitability of his coming.

And so, on Friday, May 21, 2010, in the late morning, my racehorse arrived.

Mark and Alison pulled up at our yard with their trailer. They got out cheerily and began to unfasten the side door. I was in a state of nervous anticipation, a sickly feeling in my stomach. We could see a long, orange head staring out from within the trailer. Mark attached the head collar and lead rope to it and began to advance. Herman followed. He bounded athletically down the ramp and clattered on to the road, before standing still, drawing himself up to his full height, snorting and looking around at his new surroundings.

"Oh my God!" said Jenny.

I looked in amazement as Mark brought him on to the yard and marched him into his stable, carefully prepared with a big bed of straw and a net of fresh haylage. Mark slipped off the head collar and unfastened the horse's travel boots, and we watched as Herman began making anxious bustling circuits of the stable, pausing now and again to dash to the door for a worried look outside. He kept on the move, his eyes wide and rolling.

Herman had arrived with his saddle and bridle and a blue plastic crate of belongings, including the furry pad and the gold fly rug and hat. We stored his stuff away, made sure he was comfortable and left him to his anxious pacing in the hope that he would soon settle in.

We waved off Mark and Alison and watched as their vehicle drove away, pulling the now empty trailer. My thoughts turned to what had been in it, the big orange racehorse in Baby's old stable. My racehorse. Now I had got it, what was I going to do with it?

I returned to look over the stable door. Herman nibbled at his haynet, then continued his pacing. He looked at me out of the corner of his rolling eye, but did not meet my gaze. I wondered what to make of him. It was hard to know yet. He seemed worried, but that was understandable, having just arrived at a strange place. He was on his toes, but that too was to be expected. There was an air of vulnerability and pent-up emotion about him. I was getting the feeling of a soul in need.

I was entranced by him. Already, I felt this was a horse I could bond with, that he could really and truly be my horse.

I decided I wanted my own name for my own horse. To me he wasn't a Herman Monster. I thought about his racing name, Adelphi Warrior. It sounded Greek. Indeed, 'adelphi' derives from a Greek word meaning brother. I like ancient history and

I have a book about the most famous Greek warrior of them all, who conquered Europe and Asia and rode into battle on his beloved horse, Bucephalus. He became known as 'The Great.'

There could be only one name for my own 'great' horse. I called him Alexander.

Alexander racing at Witton Castle
(Grossick Racing Photography)

Chapter Five

To Race Or Not To Race?

By February of 2017 I was indulging myself with a childhood dream. I wanted to ride in a race. And the charity Flat race at Skipton seemed to have our names on it. For the first time in my life, I could completely focus on preparing for such an event. I could never have got Alexander, or myself, race fit when arriving at the yard from work in the dark winter evenings five days a week. Redundancy meant I could train us to take part.

The charity race is a popular annual event at Skipton and raises thousands of pounds for good causes. I had watched it the previous year and been moved by the pure joy of hobby riders similar to me crossing the finishing line on a wide variety of horses, from chunky cobs and big Clydesdales to sleek thoroughbreds. For some, winning was important but for most, taking part was all that mattered. Jenny had suggested that I took Alexander next time. It was an intriguing prospect but the idea soon faded from my mind.

A year on, the decision to race was an easy one. I felt it was now or never. Alexander was a racing veteran at thirteen years old, while I was pushing sixty. This could be our only chance to race together. As I told friends: "We've a combined age of over seventy, so we need to get on with it!"

I thought Jenny might have gone off the idea, but she remained supportive.

"Go for it," she said. "It's your dream. The thought of you racing over fences terrifies me, but this is a Flat race."

Alexander was typically laid back about it.

"How would you feel about going racing again?" I asked him as he munched on a haynet in his stable. He broke off briefly to eye me suspiciously and then went back to eating.

For years I had agonised about taking Alexander back to the racetrack. Always before, my courage had deserted me.

He had been a steeplechaser, so when I first considered the idea it seemed natural that I should look at point-to-point racing. But my enthusiasm evaporated when I saw the steeplechase fences close up. They were a huge 4ft 6ins in height. I stood next to one and it came up to my chest. The fence sloped away on the take-off side, making it very wide as well as very high. I couldn't see how I would ever be brave enough to gallop Alexander at such an obstacle.

But the burning desire refused to go away and Ian Conroy was never slow to feed the flames. One day, when we were having a meal out, he asked: "Why don't you take Alexander round Whittington point-to-point?"

"I think that's a bit out of our league," I replied.

"He'll go round, no problem," Ian assured me.

"Yes, I'm sure he would, but I don't think I could," I said.

"Why not? What you are doing now with him, showjumping and the rest, is harder than galloping at those steeplechase fences and jumping them out of stride. He'll just take you over them."

A twinkle came into Ian's eye and he grinned across the table: "You'll be fine. Just shut your eyes, hold on to his mane and pull him up before the open ditch! It doesn't matter about winning, what's important is having a go. You'll always regret it if you don't."

Ian had hit a nerve and he knew it. I didn't want any more regrets in my life. I had battled too many demons to go to my grave with 'if only' on my lips. And although the message was delivered with a smile, I knew he was deadly serious.

"Maybe we could do it," I said.

Ian said Alexander would need six to eight weeks training to get him race fit. In the last two weeks, I would have to school him over steeplechase fences.

"I know Jimmy Moffatt. He's a professional trainer just up the road from us," Ian said.

"Jimmy and his dad, Dudley, recommended Alexander to us when he was a youngster at the breeder's farm. I'm sure he'll let you use his gallops and he'll give you good advice as well. Come on, I'll show you them."

Jenny and I were lunching with Ian and Karen at a restaurant near their stud farm at Grange-over-Sands. We were at our favourite table by the window, with views over the hilly, wooded countryside to Morecambe Bay. As the ladies ordered a second bottle of white wine, Ian and I fastened our coats and ventured out into the cold drizzle.

In five minutes, Ian had driven us to the pretty village of Cartmel.

"That's where you'd canter round to warm up," he said, as we passed a small railed circuit.

We drove through the village and took a quiet road out of it.

"That's the Moffatts' yard across the fields," said Ian, pointing through the murk to a cluster of farm buildings. "The gallops are just coming up on the right."

I peered through the now driving rain, eager for my first glimpse of the training gallops. We pulled into the side of the road, got out of the car and looked at the hillside. I could see the track where the racehorses were trained. It climbed until it seemed almost vertical as it disappeared into the distance. It then veered sharp left before rising again towards the top of the steep and bleak fell. In the next field, I could see a line of daunting steeplechase fences and a few hurdles.

"The gallops are a mile and a half long," Ian said. "If Jimmy helps, he will ride one of his fastest racehorses ahead of you. If you and Alexander are still just a few yards behind when you get to the top, he will be fit enough for pointing."

The vision of me charging up that hill behind Jimmy Moffatt suddenly became all too clear. I said nothing but my thoughts were tumbling wildly. I probably wouldn't have the bottle, or the stickability, to jump those enormous fences, but I had the horse to do it.

I was touched by Ian's faith in me, and he knew what he was talking about. Although very modest about his riding achievements, Ian raced as a jump jockey under National Hunt rules some thirty years ago. He rode at Chepstow and Haydock and raced in America, winning in Pennsylvania. Karen has a framed photograph of him receiving a trophy from an elegant lady in a big hat and long gloves.

Back at the pub, Ian said: "You can do it. I know you can. And it would be a privilege if you would let me lead Alexander round the paddock before the race."

I knew the offer was genuine and I was moved. Ian always claimed he had not ridden since the day Alexander reversed at speed back to the yard as he tried to take him down the lane at the stud farm.

"He must really think we are worth it," I thought.

I smiled: "The job is yours and I hope you'll lead him into the Winners' Enclosure afterwards."

Ian couldn't resist a quip.

"When you choose your racing colours, don't pick green – we won't be able to see you when you're on the ground!"

We laughed, but a mad idea had grown legs and started to run. Knowing how dangerous the desire to race Alexander was, I had locked it away. But I still had the key and sometimes it unlocked the door and the desire got out. It had escaped again.

It was an exciting plan but it never came to fruition. In the sober light of day my bravado disappeared. My head overruled my heart and I locked the desire away again.

Now the urge had returned. And in the guise of a Flat race, it seemed more realistic.

In the past, friends had warned that going back to racing could blow Alexander's brain and ruin years of hard work to make him a safe ride.

But he was now a mature, settled and very happy horse. I felt he would cope with being back on the racetrack.

Some years before, I had been given a unique insight into Alexander the racehorse by Richard Smith, the young jockey who rode him in his two races.

I had bumped into Richard at Skipton Races in 2013. Auroras Encore, who had won the Grand National a month earlier, was due to parade but he was unable to be there. As I bought a race programme, I joked: "I should have brought my own racehorse instead."

"What's he called?" asked Michelle, in charge of programme sales.

"You won't have heard of him."

"Try me."

"Adelphi Warrior."

She looked at me.

"You must be Steve."

Michelle had bought my first book, *Run With Your Heart*. It seemed strange that someone I had not met knew both me and my horse. But it was a nice feeling.

I must have got carried away by it. Minutes later, a teenager looked in my direction and shouted: "Have you sold many?"

"Quite a few,"I yelled back, not recognising him and trying to work out where I must know him from. Then a woman's voice came from behind me. She was clutching a tray of buns and calling to the boy, who was clearly her son: "There's some left."

Red-faced, I shuffled quickly off to the burger van.

When Richard's name was announced among the runners and riders for the final race, I thought I was hearing things. He was a huge link to Alexander's racing past and I had to speak to him.

I watched from a distance as he talked to the horse's owners following the race and then disappeared into the jockeys' tent. I gave him time to change before sending in a message asking to see him. A few seconds later he emerged and looked quizzically at me.

"Can I help?"

"I'm sorry to bother you, but I think you rode my horse,"I began, feeling lost for words and slightly foolish, like a youngster seeking an autograph.

Richard was polite but appeared a little perplexed.

"It was three years ago. He's a chestnut called Adelphi Warrior."

Richard's brow furrowed. Clearly there was no instant recollection.

I bumbled on.

"I think you rode him for Carol or Caroline Dennis."

His brow became slightly less furrowed.

"Caroline,"he said. "I still ride for her sometimes. But I can't quite remember…"

"He raced against Hunt Ball,"I proffered in desperation.

A sudden light of recognition came into Richard's eyes.

"Didn't he run at Witton Castle?"

"Yes,"I gasped.

"He came from Martin Todhunter's yard."

"That's right!"

"And he had orange racing colours."

"Yes, he did, he did."

My God, he remembers riding my horse!

The information was flowing fast now.

"His second race was at Dalston," said Richard. "We thought he would run well but he just didn't perform that day. The ground was soft and sticky and he didn't go on it."

He added: "I rather liked him."

By now I was bursting with pride. It was like listening to a teacher praising your child.

Richard had to dash back to the north east but he gave me his number and said we could talk again when there was more time. He was as good as his word when I called him a couple of weeks later, happily chatting about Alexander for half an hour.

Richard, whose grandfather Denys Smith trained Red Alligator to win the Grand National in 1968, was only twenty one and starting out as a jockey when he rode Alexander. He was introduced to him by point-to-point trainer Chris Dennis.

"Chris brought him down to my place and asked if I would have a sit on him and see if he was any good. I popped him over a couple of fences and he jumped them nicely. I was happy enough, so I rode him at Witton Castle.

"There were a handful of runners in the race. A few of the horses hadn't raced before and we went a really steady pace.

"I just looked after him and got him jumping. He jumped well but he wasn't quick between his fences. But he felt all right and he kept going. I didn't have to chase him along until we went into the home straight. Then they went flat out. He went with them for a bit and then faded. I thought he ran quite well, to say he hadn't run before.

"At Dalston, the ground was a bit softer. There were more runners and they went more of a gallop. He still jumped well but he struggled on the ground. I pulled him up two fences from the finish.

"I didn't know what happened to him after that. It was hard to tell after two races if he would have taken to it. But I wouldn't have knocked him back. I thought there was something there.

"Horses bred by Alflora don't tend to be the quickest, but they keep going. They also develop later, so he could still have been weak."

Richard's final comments struck a chord.

"Some horses you don't know how much you can trust. But I felt he would look after us. I felt he wouldn't do anything daft. He wouldn't be looking for a way out, or chuck me off down at the start.

"He was laid back, perhaps too laid back for racing. He was a grand horse."

Recalling those remarks gave me the confidence that I was making the right decision in taking Alexander back to the track.

Chapter Six

Festival Of Dreams

My racing dream took on new meaning when I first saw Alexander's relatives running at the prestigious Cheltenham Festival. It got me thinking seriously about the wonderful athlete I was lucky enough to ride.

Over four days in March, more than 250,000 race fans flock to the Cheltenham course for one of the biggest national sporting events of the year. Millions more watch on TV. I was one. I didn't miss a race and loved every minute of the action. But how could watching the Festival at home match the thrill of actually being there? I wanted to be part of that huge throng of people, to add to the clamorous roar from the stands, and to be close to the famous Queen Mother statue when the victors were led into the Winners' Enclosure.

I had never had the time or the money to go but in 2014, I finally made it. It was literally a busman's holiday, a coach trip with other racegoers from Yorkshire to the last two days of the Festival. The cost of £320, for myself and Jenny, covered travel; dinner, bed and breakfast at a three-star hotel; and entry to the races, including the Cheltenham Gold Cup. When the tour company asked to pick us up at Bradford instead of Skipton, I negotiated a £40 reduction in price. Less than £300 seemed a small price to pay. Then the letter from the holiday company arrived, confirming the booking.

"Bloody 'ell!" I exclaimed, as I eagerly scanned the details. "We've got to be in Bradford at 4.30am."

It made sense, of course. It's a long way from Yorkshire to Cheltenham. I had been too excited about our trip to count the hours backwards from the start of the first race to when we would have to set off. But the unholiness of the hour did not dampen my enthusiasm and when the phone alarm shrilled at 3am, I sprang out of bed. This was World Hurdle day at the Festival and in twelve hours we would be there to watch it!

A little over an hour later, we pulled into a deserted car park in the centre of Bradford. Bang on time, a big coach loomed out of the darkness and pulled up. The driver ticked off the eight passengers on his list, loaded our suitcases and ushered us on board.

"Can you sit at the back?" he asked. "It will be easier when we make the rest of the pick-ups."

There seemed no reason to object and we settled into comfortable seats three rows from the rear. By the time we had collected another group from Leeds, two things had become apparent. Firstly, nearly all our holiday companions were male. Secondly, some were already in robust party mood. Before the next stop, in Wakefield, I heard a metallic rip, followed by a fizz. The chap two rows in front had opened his first can of strong lager. It was 5am. By the time we got to Barnsley, his pals had followed suit, tearing into can after can until the coach smelled like a brewery. The bloke immediately in front of us was an exception - his preferred dawn tipple was red wine. He swigged from a constant succession of small glass bottles and when we reached our scheduled breakfast stop, at Tibshelf Services in Derbyshire, his bag was clanking with 'empties.'

This was all well and good. These were hard working chaps determined to make the most of their well-earned break. What became tiresome on a journey that was to last eight hours was the constant loud diatribe on anything and everything he could think of from the bloke two seats in front of us. With no travelling companion next to him, he had to turn round to address his nearest pals, directly in front of us. Although his subjects of conversation were not wide ranging, they were inexhaustible; made more so by the fact that he repeated every sentence at least twice. We were regaled with endless shouted tales of betting, boozing and burgers. Each mini saga had an identical, bellowed conclusion.

"It wa' fuckin' shit, mate. Fuckin' shit… absolute fuckin' shit."

I didn't even have a Racing Post to bury my head in until we stopped off at Tibshelf. After that, we got stuck interminably on the M6. As we sat there for what seemed hours, our garrulous friend blocked the coach toilet by flouting the 'liquids only' regulation, to the great hilarity of his chums. This prompted hours of literal toilet humour, to the weariness of the other passengers and the exasperation of the tour guide. Stuck on the motorway with a broken toilet and in the midst of a raucous barrage of coarse jokes from alcohol swilling blokes was not the ideal start to our adventure.

After what seemed like days, we reached the outskirts of Cheltenham. By now, some of our fellow travellers had run out of steam. Several slumbered gently in a haze of alcohol fumes while others leafed quietly through The Sun's racing pages. Noisy Chap had ground to a conversational halt after his last, and lengthiest, tale about his holiday in Spain. Even the story's inevitable conclusion: "It wa' fuckin' shit, mate," seemed to lack its customary resonance.

We crept nearer to our destination, through the clinging morning mist, in an endless line of cars, taxis and coaches taking thousands of people to the racecourse. I began to anxiously check the time. There was less than an hour to the first race.

Then one of our companions chirped up: "The Army barracks are coming up on the left. It's not far from here."

Soon afterwards, we swung sharp left into a grassy car park, already crammed with row upon row of huge, gleaming coaches. Signs on their windscreens told us they had journeyed from all over the country.

"Right, we're here," announced the tour guide. "Remember where we are parked and head back to the coach as quickly as you can after the final race. Good luck and have fun!"

At last, we were stepping out into the open air. The sun was battling to pierce the heavy mist but it was thinner now and we could see where we were going, though we had no idea in which direction we should be heading.

I grabbed Jenny's hand and we plunged into the throng of people heading towards the spectacular stands of the racecourse. We crossed a heritage railway line where, a few yards up the track, a splendid black steam engine stood gently hissing. Some folk, it seemed, had enjoyed a more romantic trip to the races than us.

We were part of a moving human carpet, from ordinary folk in casual dress to toffs in posh suits and ladies in high heels, strappy dresses and fancy hats, clinging to flutes of champagne. Two older women, with worn and florid faces, appeared suddenly in front of us. They were dressed in traditional gipsy clothing and spoke with a strong Irish lilt. They purposefully blocked my path and one of them stuffed a sprig of white heather in my top pocket.

"That will bring you good luck, sir," she beamed.

"Thank you," I said, anxious to be reunited with Jenny, who had neatly sidestepped the women. I tried to dodge round them too, but the one who had given me the heather planted herself in front of me. Her mood had changed and she snarled: "Give it back!" Wanting to get away, I yanked the heather from my pocket and hurled it towards her. She plucked it two-handed out of the air, like an expert slip fielder pocketing a catch, and I scuttled past.

Jenny raised her eyebrows. "You're supposed to pay for the lucky heather."

"I didn't want the damn thing anyway," I said."Hmm," Jenny replied. "You shouldn't have upset them today if you want to pick a winner."

It was Irish Day at Cheltenham and everywhere we looked there were jolly people from the Emerald Isle in green outfits. There were also plenty of ticket touts, pleasant but persistent. At almost every step of the way someone called out: "Anyone need tickets for Tattersall's and Club?" This meant nothing to us. We had no idea of the layout of the racecourse and hadn't a clue where, or what, anything was. Our tickets were for the Best Mate Enclosure, named in honour of the three times Cheltenham Gold Cup winner. As we were swept along by the crowd, we passed a grand entrance guarded by footmen in livery. Clearly that was not our way in.

I was getting worried. There was now less than half an hour to the first race and one of my favourite horses, Double Ross, was running. I didn't want to miss seeing him.

At last we spotted 'Best Mate Enclosure' signs and, after tramping along for another ten minutes, we reached the turnstiles guarding the entrance. A helpful attendant showed us which way to insert our tickets, and we were inside.

At first, all I could see were fast food stalls and betting offices. It reminded me of a football ground as we dodged round chaps in jeans and T-shirts, swigging lager from plastic cups. Being a Yorkshire lad I ought to have felt at home, but it wasn't quite what I had expected.

"Stay close," I called to Jenny. "We don't want to lose each other."

"I can always call you if we get split up," she shouted.

"I'll never hear the phone in the middle of this lot," I yelled back.

We passed through a short tunnel and emerged at the front of the enclosure. Before us were rows of bookies with their stands. Beyond them I could see the white plastic rails and the racecourse on the other side. It was my first real view of Cheltenham and I drank in what I could. The mist was still hanging in the air and I could see only as far as the final two fences. Behind us was a concrete terrace with painted metal railings, reminding me again of the old football grounds before all-seater stadiums. At the top of the steps was a bar and a café behind a long row of glass doors and windows.

We found a space halfway up the concrete steps and I assessed our vantage point. The Best Mate Enclosure is a self-contained island on the far side of the final straight and the winning post. Gazing across at the magnificent main grandstands three hundred yards away, it suddenly dawned on me that the parade ring must be behind them. This was confirmed moments later when the runners began to emerge on to the course. I was dismayed. It meant that I would not be able to see those wonderful horses close up.

"We're in the wrong place, Jen," I said, raising my binoculars to see the horses better.

"Perhaps we can get an upgrade," she suggested.

"Yes, maybe, but I've no idea where. We'll have to find out after this race."

The runners were being cantered across the course. They swept past in front of us before disappearing into the mist.

"There's Double Ross!" I shouted, spotting a chestnut horse whose jockey was wearing his familiar scarlet and white colours. I stood in awe as he flew by and out of sight. I prayed he would come back safe.

We focused on the huge TV screen in the centre of the course which was projecting the ghostly figures of the horses circling at the start. The waiting seemed to last forever. And then a great roar went up from the stands opposite and we saw from the screen that the race had begun. Buried in the mist, the horses and riders were like spectres as they ran to the first fence at great speed. We followed the race on the screen until the runners came into eyeshot. They galloped past to begin their final circuit of the course and I was struck by how fast they were going. I saw with delight that Double Ross was in the leading three. They disappeared into the mist again, chased by a riderless horse. In what seemed no time at all, the three leaders came charging down to the final two fences. Double Ross was still there. He jumped the last and surged up the hill to the finish. The horses flew past us, locked together all the way to the line. Double Ross was narrowly beaten into third place but he had run a cracking race.

Now I turned my attention to relocating to the main stands. Although desperate to get a close-up view of the horses, I had another reason for wanting to move. Julian Brown, book publishing manager at the Racing Post, had agreed to meet me that day to talk about the possibility of publishing Run With Your Heart. The informal meeting was to be at the Racing Post Arkle Book Shop, overlooking the parade ring.

I turned to Jenny: "We've got to get over there or I'm not going to be able to see Julian."

Helpful racecourse staff directed us to the right kiosk, where we learned it would cost £14 each to upgrade. I dug deep and minutes later we were on the right side of the racetrack, thrusting our way through the crowds between the towering stands and the hospitality buildings. We passed the entrance to the Hall of Fame and finally emerged into a clearer space to find ourselves looking down on the parade ring. We cast around us, but through the masses of people we could not see what we were looking for. Then we spotted the famous statue of Arkle, looking out regally over the racecourse, and just a few yards away was the Arkle Book Shop.

It wasn't exactly a shop, more a high quality three-sided covered stall with a front counter and shelves set out with rows of beautiful horse books. I could see Ruby Walsh, Tony McCoy, Arkle and many other legendary men and horses staring back at me from among the pristine hardbacks. There were three members of staff. One was standing slightly to one side, in front of the counter. He was smallish in build, neatly dressed and looked…well, bookish. He seemed relaxed but I got the impression he didn't miss much. He had spotted me and was regarding me with a piercing but friendly gaze.

I walked briskly towards him and a warm smile lit his face.

"Steve," he said. It was a statement, not a question.

"Julian," I beamed and clasped his outstretched hand.

I took to him instantly and we chatted easily until I realised the horses were parading for the Ryanair Chase. It was a race that had particular significance for me. One of the runners was a horse called Hunt Ball who in humbler days had raced against Alexander.

"I've got to go," I said, gripping Julian's hand again.

The crowds were now so dense it was impossible to get anywhere near the parade ring so I dashed up some stairs to get a vantage point and soon picked out Hunt Ball being led round. Seeing him made me think hard about the horse I had at home, and what I wanted to do with him. But when I asked myself if I wanted to race Alexander, at however lowly a level, and if he would want to race with me, I did not readily have the answers.

We watched the race from a high point in the stands and got a great view of Hunt Ball finishing an impressive fourth.

Our first day at Cheltenham flew by. We boarded the coach

and an hour and a half later arrived at our hotel on an industrial estate just off the M5 outside Swindon. It was not the swankiest place but it was clean and comfortable. We slumped wearily into cosy armchairs in the bar and made light work of a pint of Guinness and a double gin and tonic before dinner.

The next day, the racecourse was abuzz with excitement and expectation. Helicopters hovered above the huge crowds surging to the stands, and TV crews were everywhere. It felt as if the whole world was at Cheltenham on Gold Cup day.

This time we knew where we were going. We were down to the Best Mate Enclosure in double quick time to upgrade, my wallet at the ready. But I had not taken into account that it was Gold Cup day. The serious looking old boy manning the kiosk shook his head decisively at me.

"Not today. There's no upgrades today."

"Let's walk back and see if there is another entrance we can get in," I said. "At least we might see some of the horses being led from the stables."

I had discovered where the stables were, not far from the Best Mate Enclosure. From there, the horses were led across a large yard to a tunnel and a long walkway, away from the crowds, and into the parade ring. The ticket touts were still all around, shouting out their tempting offers. As we wandered aimlessly, Jenny looked across at one of them and turned to me.

"Why don't we buy a couple of tickets?" she asked.

"I can't afford them," I said. "They'll cost a fortune."

"Look, this is your special treat. You haven't spent your money on anything else."

I stood contemplating. The tout saw us hovering and was instantly at our side.

"Need tickets?"

We looked at each other uncertainly.

"Is it for Club or Tattersall's?"

"Er, Club," ventured Jenny.

"We can't afford that," I interjected. "How much are Tattersall's?"

"I tell you what, I'll do you two tickets for £150."

"Too much. I can't do it."

The tout, a casually smart young man, thought quickly and revised the offer. But again, I declined. It might be a dream shattered but there had to be some common sense.

The tout hadn't given up.

"I tell you what," he repeated. "I'll do you two tickets for £80."

Jenny and I looked at each other questioningly. Slowly, I opened my wallet and handed over the money. The tout pushed two tickets into my hand. They had Tattersall's printed on them and seemed genuine enough. I looked across at the electric turnstiles.

"They are going to work, aren't they?"

"Yes. Don't worry. I'm not going anywhere. You'll see I'm still here."

We strolled to the turnstiles, trying to look nonchalant. I was terribly afraid that we had just blown £80.

A man just ahead of us in the queue stopped at the barrier. A security man came forward. There was a problem.

"Oh God! That's going to be us," I thought.

We joined another queue. Jenny was in front. She was unsure which way the ticket went in. Another security man stepped forward to help. He took hold of the ticket.

"This is where we get thrown out," I thought.

But the ticket went in the slot and Jenny was ushered through. I held my breath as I stuck my ticket in the barrier and prayed silently that it too would work.

A green light flashed. "Come through," said the security man.

It was the busiest day of the week and the place was heaving. We passed the book shop and I marched to the steps leading to the excellent vantage point where we had watched most of the races the previous day. I was about to put my foot on the first step when a liveried official barred my way. I showed him my ticket.

"You can't go in there," he announced grimly.

"But we did yesterday."

"Not today," he replied icily.

"Of course. Gold Cup day."

He nodded sternly.

I dashed around looking for other entrances. Each one admitted Club standard tickets only. Tattersall's got you into one area on Gold Cup day - Tattersall's. That enclosure was accessed via a huge bar, so jam-packed it was hardly possible to put one foot in front of the other. I battled for five minutes to get through to the narrow terrace on the other side where people were standing three deep. It was almost impossible to see the course, so I turned round and headed back.

"This is hopeless," I said. "We're never going to get a good view."

"Why don't we just stay around the parade ring?" said Jenny. "We can get close to the horses before and after, and watch the races on the big screen. We'll see much more that way."

It was inspired, and that is precisely what we did. Most people were in the stands or the bars during the actual races, so we could get right down to the front in the paddock, next to the horses as they were paraded round before the jockeys got on them. And afterwards, we were right there when the winner and placed horses came back, to the cheers of the crowds, and the presentations took place. I was in my element as I got close-up views of some of my favourite racehorses. The wonderful athletes were lean and mean and super fit. Most were smaller than Alexander and looked very different from him.

The Festival was drawing to a close when a horse called Pearlysteps entered the parade ring. He and Alexander had the same father. He was almost level with us before I made out his number. I nudged Jenny excitedly and burst out: "It's Pearlysteps!"

He was no more than ten feet in front of us. He looked great but I found myself thinking protectively: "He doesn't look as magnificent as Alexander."

There were more than twenty runners in the race but Pearlysteps ran well to finish fourth. Somehow, I missed him before he was led back to the stables so I dashed off and sneaked past the security guards, trying my best to look like a racehorse trainer in my suit, overcoat and checked cap. As I scuttled to the long walkway and tunnel, I saw a stable lass carrying a saddle and black and white colours. She passed someone who shouted: "Congratulations! Your lad ran well."

"Thank you," she smiled, and hurried on towards the stables.

I shuffled up alongside her.

"Who's your lad?" I asked.

"Pearlysteps."

I had half expected the answer but I was still delighted.

"Fantastic," I said. "He's related to my horse."

The stable lass naturally had other things on her mind but she generously put up with me as I fell into stride with her and rabbited away for the next couple of minutes. When we approached the entrance to the stables, she stopped for a moment. "You can't go any further," she said.

"I understand. Please take these," and I shoved two posters for my book into her spare hand.

She looked bewildered. "What do you want me to do with these?"

"Whatever you like. Chuck them away if you want, but your lad is mentioned in the book."

She nodded and turned away with the saddle.

"Give him an extra pat from me," I called after her.

"Will do."

My Cheltenham dream was now at an end. I had blown the office Fantasy Football prize money on my Orange Accumulator, a self-invented bet involving chestnut horses, and would have to dig deep into my own pocket at the end of the soccer season to replace the money entrusted to me by my work colleagues. But my two days at the Festival had been unforgettable. Seeing such magnificent horses was magical. And getting so close to Pearlysteps made me dream again of the horse and jockey that could be Alexander and me.

Twelve months later we were back at Cheltenham. This time it was for all four days of the Festival and it did not involve a 4am start or a coach load of drinkers.

Instead, we drove down the day before. After a lot of searching on the internet, I had found us somewhere to stay within a fifteen-minute walk of the racecourse. It was a traditional guest house with high ceilings, huge windows and lots of stairs. The cheerful landlady had run it for many years and kept it going for a handful of race-going regulars. On the eve of the Festival, we strolled through the genteel streets of Cheltenham to see what was going on. In my case, it was more of a hobble. The week before, I was struck down with gout. The big toe joint of my right foot was so inflamed I couldn't get my shoe on, and I had to take time off work. They say gout is caused by rich living, but that certainly wasn't the case with me

"I have never lived so abstemiously," I complained.

Anti-inflammatory pills had made it easier, but I was still limping badly.

Dusk was falling as we passed the large 'Welcome to Cheltenham Racecourse' signs and the great grandstands loomed up in front of us. We were able to see down one side of the course. The fences and hurdles disappeared into the distance, like silent sentinels in the gathering gloom. We were on the cusp of the great event and the atmosphere was alive with huge expectation. Several horse wagons, mostly from Ireland, were already parked up. Some of the horses were being walked out and I felt a buzz of anticipation. We made our way into the town centre and had a drink at the oldest pub in Cheltenham, dating back to the 1660s, before heading back to the guest house. We wanted an early night in readiness for the excitement of the next day. But what should have been a straightforward ten minute walk turned into a frustrating and wearying marathon when I plunged off in the wrong direction.

"I'm sure we should be going that way," said Jenny, pointing to the left.

"No, no," I insisted. "It's right here, and then we'll be nearly there."

We plodded on miserably, down endless residential streets, until I finally had to admit that we were completely lost.

"We're going to be walking round all night," Jenny complained.

I couldn't argue.

Eventually, we flagged down a passing taxi and I guiltily forked out for the fare. Despite our interminable meanderings, we were only a couple of minute's drive from the guest house. We got back exhausted, my swollen foot throbbing painfully in protest.

It was all forgotten the next morning as I excitedly tuned into Channel Four's Morning Line. It was broadcast live from the course and the images of the horses exercising brought home how close we were to our big adventure.

We set off after breakfast. The weather was fine and the walk pleasant. Hundreds of people were heading on foot in the same direction and battalions of huge coaches rumbled past.

By just after 10am, we had reached the course. The gates were not yet open but the next half hour proved to be one of the highlights of the week. We stood at the rail overlooking the entrance to the stables as wagons and trailers pulled up and the racehorses were unloaded. It was spellbinding to watch these beautiful animals emerge, their devoted grooms patting and talking to them as they led them to the stables. We made sure we were there every day and were rewarded by seeing some of our favourite horses arrive. The best thing about Cheltenham is being able to get so close to the horses. You can almost touch them as they march past in the parade ring, are led into the Winners' Enclosure, or are washed off with buckets of water after a race. It is only when you are so near to them in the flesh that you can truly appreciate how stunning they are.

When the entrance gates opened, we walked to the rail next to the winning post. I stood and gazed across the course, stretching immaculately away into the distance. It was bathed in sunshine.

All was ready. The waiting was almost over.

Jenny sat on a bench on The Lawn in front of the main grandstand. You wouldn't be able to move on there in a couple of hours. I was chatting to a couple of stewards guarding a gate to the racetrack when I had to move aside to let top jockey Barry Geraghty through. He had just finished walking the course.

Fellow jockey Ruby Walsh had a remarkable first day, winning three of the first four races, including the Champion Hurdle. He seemed set for a fourth win, on the exciting chestnut mare, Annie Power, when she came crashing down at the final hurdle. She got straight to her feet and galloped away.

But a second mare, L'Unique, also fell, and she stayed down. I was watching from the grandstand and saw her raise her head. Within seconds, a vet was with her and gently lowered her head to the turf. Then the dreaded green screens were erected and she was hidden from view.

The screens are put up to allow the vets to work on an injured horse in privacy and to keep the animal calm. It doesn't necessarily mean a horse has been seriously injured, but you always fear the worst.

I did not see who won the race. My eyes were fixed on the green screens, and I prayed silently that the mare would be all right. Five long minutes went by. Suddenly, the screens were removed and there she was, on her feet. A huge cheer erupted from the grandstand as we all roared our approval. L'Unique had only been winded. Applause rang out as she was led jauntily away, none the worse for her fall. She got a bigger reception than the winner of the race. It was a measure of how much these racehorses are loved. We celebrate them just as much when they survive as when they succeed.

That was probably the best moment of the week for me. But it was almost matched on the first day before the racing had even begun. A parade of retired racehorses is held every year, heralding the start of the Festival. We were able to get to the front of the parade ring as former jumping stars were ridden round, including Kauto Star, Denman and Big Buck's, and they all looked magnificent. It was a privilege to see them and it brought tears to my eyes. It was a particular delight to see Kauto Star. He was a stunning looking racehorse, and in my opinion the greatest steeplechaser since the legendary Arkle.

This time I was at Cheltenham as a published author. Run With Your Heart had been produced as a paperback by Racing Post Books the previous September. It was exciting to see copies of my book on display at the Racing Post Book Shop, alongside those of AP McCoy and Clare Balding.

"Do you want to sign a few copies?" one of the staff asked. "We can put a 'signed' sticker on and it helps to sell them."

He placed a pile of my books on the counter. At that moment, a smartly dressed lady approached, intent on purchasing a form guide booklet. As she waited to pay for it, she picked up the book on top of the pile and glanced at the cover. I waited for a few seconds and then, in the politest manner I could muster, said to her: "Would you like a signed copy, madam?"

I didn't expect a positive response but the lady looked more closely at the blurb on the back cover and replied: "I think I will, it looks interesting." That flustered me. Having a book in print still felt alien. The lady watched in expectation as my pen hovered over the inside cover. I was unsure what should happen next.

"What message would you like?" I asked uncertainly.

She replied: "Just put 'Penny, with best wishes' - and don't forget to sign your name!"

I did as she asked, adding 'Steve' with a flourish.

It was my first book signing and I asked the staff member to take a photo on my phone. It showed my shiny bald head and Penny's broad-brimmed hat bending over the book, but it captured a moment.

I had brought along a couple of home-made posters advertising the book, and I handed one of them to Mrs Diana Whateley, the owner of Wishfull Thinking, another horse with the same father as Alexander. I called him Alexander's 'best brother' and it was a thrill to see him, even though he was unplaced in his race. When he had been washed down and led away, I noticed his owner walking towards me. I knew it was cheeky, but I couldn't resist.

"Mrs Whateley?" I said.

She stopped and smiled: "Yes."

"I'm sorry to intrude, but I'm a big fan of your horse."

Her face lit up with pride.

Mrs Whateley must have had far more important things to do than chit-chat with me on a chilly afternoon. But she didn't show it. She seemed genuinely interested when I told her about Alexander and my book, and how her horse was mentioned in it. She stood for ten minutes as we talked about our horses. When I told her that I competed on Alexander, she smiled and said: "You're very lucky to ride a horse like that. Good for you!"

I'd had a modest bet on Wishfull Thinking and lost my money. More frustrating was my failure to back the only other 'brother' running at the Festival. I still punched the air and shouted him home as Darna jumped the last fence in front, and held on to win at long odds.

I am far more interested in seeing the horses than having a bet. I have a modest flutter on some of the races, and winning is a bonus. But Cheltenham 2015 was a much bigger success than the year before. I was already slightly ahead for the week when it came to my final bets on the Gold Cup. I plumped for the outstanding novice Coneygree, and the big Irish hope, Djakadam, with Ruby Walsh riding, and watched in amazement as they finished first and second. I won £115 on the race and ended up with one winner, three seconds and a third from seven each way bets.

We celebrated with a drink in the Istabraq Bar and I spent some of my winnings on a meal at a Thai restaurant in the centre of Cheltenham. It was in sharp contrast to evenings earlier in the week when we had dined on sandwiches from Morrisons and fish and chips on a park bench.

Our journey home seemed to go on forever and eventually we pulled into a service station for a break. I realised it was Tibshelf Services - the same place where we had stopped with our rowdy coach party a year before.

This time I felt able to relax. We sat at a table, tired but happy, and munched on sandwiches and sipped Costa coffees.

I couldn't resist buying a copy of the Racing Post. The front page headline was 'Fairytale', referring to the victory of Coneygree. But it could just as easily have been talking about me. Being at the racing festival had underlined that my journey with Alexander was my very own fairytale.

Seeing those magnificent racehorses emphasised how lucky I was to have my own.

Next to the Best Mate statue at Cheltenham

Chapter Seven

Back In Training

It was a simple task to enter the charity race.

As usual, the local Hunt organised the point-to-point meeting, which was held on private farmland, with rolling hills, just outside the North Yorkshire market town of Skipton. The Flat race, in aid of the children's cancer charity Candlelighters, would be run before the steeplechasing. It was on the same course but avoiding the great big fences. Any rider could take part, but they had to raise at least £250 in sponsorship money.

The first step was to pay the £50 entry fee and get the sponsorship forms. I pinned one up on the wooden wall in the toilet block at our livery yard, along with a photo of Alexander jumping a fence in his racing days. On it I had written the plea: "Please make a dream come true for two old boys!"

I was worried that I would not be able to reach the sponsorship target. Asking people for money, however worthy the cause, can be challenging. Three years ago, I had raised £200 for the New Beginnings racehorse rehabilitation charity by selling a calendar. Jenny had selected twelve seasonal horsey photos taken by ourselves and friends, and had a hundred calendars with envelopes printed. Alexander and I, standing on the hills above our yard, adorned the front cover. The back cover showed a photo of him racing. I was responsible for the hard sell and no work colleague, or professional person I came into contact with in my job, was safe from me and my carrier bag of calendars.

But this was different. There was no end product to sell. Just me, my horse and our dream.

"Don't worry," said Jenny. "If you can't raise enough money, we'll make up the deficit ourselves, so you will take part in the race."

Sue Dinsdale got us off to a flying start – despite Alexander prancing sideways up a steep hill with her during a lively hack out. Two days after I entered the race, she turned up at the yard to ride him.

"Here you are," she said, handing over a plastic envelope. Inside was £50 she had collected from family and friends. All of a sudden, we were a fifth of the way to our target!

Now I could turn my mind to training Alexander. We had nine weeks to get ready for the race. Alexander was already fit because we competed regularly in hunter trials and one-day events. He was used to running round cross-country courses, but he would have to gallop non-stop for one and a quarter miles in the race. He had not done anything like that for seven years and I had no idea what I would need to do to get him race fit. Fortunately, I knew plenty of people to ask.

"You've got to be fair to the horse," Ian Conroy said.

"If you want to give him the best chance to be competitive, you need to start a six days a week training regime immediately. Do some walking out one day, trotting up hills the next and some fast canter work the day after that. Repeat the cycle, then you can both have a day off.

"Canter him for distances up to a mile, but no more than that, and throw in a bit of gallop work. Get him into a nice rhythm in canter, ask him to quicken up for a short distance, then bring him back.

"Increase the faster work as you go. You want him to be

blowing and to have white stuff in his nostrils, or the work isn't doing any good, he won't be getting any fitter. You will have to be strict. It's no good thinking 'I won't bother today' because it's windy or rainy."

Ian added: "As you get him fitter, you might find that his attitude changes. He could get more lively."

Ian had given me plenty to think about, but he wasn't finished.

"I'm concerned about Alexander galloping for more than a mile in that big leather jumping saddle of yours. We've got one you can use. It's bigger than a racing saddle, but it's still small and light. It fits any horse and we used to ride him in it. And I'll get you some proper jockey silks to wear. If the pair of you are going to play at being a racehorse and jockey for the day, you're going to have to look the part!"

Another ex-jockey friend, Keith Rosier, who had given me his racing body protector, now offered me the use of the breast girth his racehorses had worn. And Keith reminded me that it wasn't just my horse that would have to be fit.

"If you are going to ride like a jockey, you will have to get your legs very strong. You need to do lots of trotting while standing up in the stirrups. And any hill work will be good for both of you."

I had no idea how many horses would be in the race, or how good the opposition would be, but local point-to-point rider David Coates had no doubt that Alexander would be fast enough.

"He will have no trouble galloping round that course. He has a big engine. When you press the buttons, you'll find yourself going as quick as you would ever have wanted to."

It was a thrilling, if scary, thought.

I did know about one race rival. The head girl at our yard, Emilly Thane, had entered her long-term loan horse, Joe. He was a fast, part-thoroughbred, cross-country machine and although now twenty-one, he was still the picture of gleaming, muscled health. Emilly was a strong and talented rider. It would also be her racing debut but they would be tough opponents.

Race training was an entirely new experience for me, and despite all the good advice I was getting, I was to some extent stumbling around in the dark. I was responsible for putting Alexander back in training after seven years off the track and it was down to me to decide how quickly we should build up our work, and at what point to rein it in as race day approached. If we were going to be training six days a week, I wouldn't be able to keep nagging other people for advice. I would have to trust to my instincts.

"You know your horse," Ian said. "You'll be able to feel him change. He'll tell you how fit he is."

It made sense to begin steadily and to gradually build up the level of work we were doing. Fortunately, our livery yard had just about everything I needed. I had assumed I would need to go elsewhere to get Alexander fit for our big day but as it turned out, apart from two trips to all-weather gallops, I was able to do all the work at home.

We have kept our horses at Farfield Farm Livery Centre, between Ilkley and Skipton on the edge of the Yorkshire Dales, for almost three years. It is run by Jane Barker and her stepson, Charles. Jane is petite and pretty, with bright blue eyes and her blonde hair tied in a ponytail. Her slender frame belies her strength and brisk energy and enthusiasm. Charles is a handsome young man in his late twenties, always suntanned, with short, golden hair. He is slim, but wiry and strong and nothing much phases him.

The former dairy farm has rolling acres of upland pasture,

bounded by high stone walls, with magnificent views from the hilltops across to Bolton Abbey and the famous Cow and Calf rock formation above Ilkley. The land provides riders with plenty of safe, off-road hacking along tracks and across fields.

The area is a hugely popular tourist destination and in 2014 the eyes of the world were on it when the Tour de France cycle race passed through Ilkley. Tens of thousands of people flocked to see the competitors peddling madly through the spectacular landscape on the steep and twisting North Yorkshire roads. Although the race had passed through the area a few days before we arrived at Farfield, there was still a carnival atmosphere locally, with decorated yellow bicycles, bunting and welcome posters everywhere.

One huge advantage of keeping the horses at Farfield is that Jane, Charles and their team of cheerful and highly dedicated members of staff do all the work. The horses are mucked out, turned out, brought in and fed. After we moved there, those dark, freezing cold winter evenings when we faced at least an hour's toil at the stables after a long day in Bradford became a thing of the past. I had more time to ride and that led to greater success competing and gave me the confidence to enter the race.

Having said that, we had been at our previous yard for seven years and the decision to move was not taken lightly. Although he loves it at Farfield and is a very happy horse, we were concerned at the time that Alexander might miss his old home and friends. He is a quirky horse, very prone to injury and can exhibit odd and unusual behaviour traits.

The evening before we moved to Farfield, he gave us a terrible fright when I was preparing to turn him out for the night. The flies were particularly bad, so I sprayed him with an insect repellent to try to keep them at bay. Being careful to avoid his face, I squirted the spray down his neck and flanks as he stood quietly in the middle of his stable. Suddenly, his knees buckled and he began to stagger like a drunk. Then, slowly and deliberately, he lowered himself to the floor and sank into the straw. He lay on his side, looking up at me with big eyes and making strange little peffing sounds. I looked anxiously down at him.

"Alexander, what is it?"

He stared up at me and continued to peff.

"Wait there! I'll be back in a minute!" I told him, glancing back at the prostrate orange figure, before running through the big barn to find Jenny.

"Come quickly, something awful has happened!" I shouted, waving my arms desperately.

I hoped that when I got back to his stable he would be back on his feet. But he was still in the same position, his flanks gently heaving as he made puffing noises.

Jenny appeared and she too stared down at the prone Alexander.

"Oh my God! What's happened to him?" she said.

"I don't know. What do we do?" I asked, really beginning to panic.

Was he starting to colic, or having some sort of sudden catastrophic seizure?

"We've got to get him up," said Jenny. "I can't believe it. Our last night at the yard – and this!"

Everyone else had left for the evening. We were alone with this baffling and frightening problem.

"Come on, Alexander, get up, come on!" Jenny shouted.

We waved our arms at him, clapped our hands and prodded his bottom. After a few seconds he shuffled around in the straw, and to our huge relief, dragged himself to his feet. He stood there silently, looking sorry for himself.

"Get his head collar on. Let's get him outside," said Jenny.

Once on the yard, he seemed to revive.

"Why don't we see if he'll walk up to his field?" I suggested.

We led him carefully up the stony track and he picked at the grass on the way. That was a good sign. He walked up positively and we took him through the gate into his big meadow. Immediately, his knees started to buckle and he tried to lower himself down in the muddy gateway dotted with big stones.

"No! Stay on your feet," ordered Jenny, dragging him forward towards the grass.

Alexander began to graze, swishing his tail. We removed the head collar and anxiously watched as he ate the grass for several minutes. He seemed to be acting normally. Then he lowered himself to the ground and lay there, pulling faces at us. A sickening premonition of doom sat in our stomachs as we watched him for a few seconds. Then Jenny marched up to him.

"What's the matter with you? Get up, why don't you?"

Alexander gave her a black look and reluctantly hauled himself to his feet. He sauntered off and began grazing again. It was the most extraordinarily odd behaviour. We could not make any sense of it.

"Let's ring Nick, see what he thinks," I said.

Jenny phoned our vet Nick Johnson on his mobile. He wasn't on duty and we didn't expect him to answer, but he did. The clopping of hooves in the background suggested he was out riding his own event horse but he listened carefully as Jenny told him about Alexander's strange antics.

"What's he doing now?" Nick asked.

"Well, he's just grazing."

"And how does he seem?"

"Just normal at the moment. He's with his friends, grazing and swishing his tail."

"I really can't think there's anything wrong with him," Nick concluded. "But give me a call if anything else happens."

He added politely: "He's a very interesting horse."

In the months before his mysterious collapse, Alexander had behaved in an unusual and sometimes downright odd way. He had always been content to come in from the field in the morning during the summer months, tuck into his breakfast, have a nibble of hay and enjoy a comfortable nap. We would turn up later to find an Alexander-shaped depression in his straw bed. That year was different. He had the call of the wild, refusing to stand in his stable in the day. He stressed at the door, weaving his head frantically, crossing his jaw and sticking out his tongue. The first time we saw him doing it, we thought something was horribly wrong. We had left him with a cosy bed and a bulging net of haylage but when we arrived back, he threw himself around the front of his stable, making strange gulping movements. He tipped his grooming tools on the floor and appeared to be extremely distressed. Jenny was convinced he had swallowed something from out of his grooming bucket.

"Oh God! He's choking. Get the emergency vet!" she shouted.

"I'll take him outside," I said, trying to soothe him.

I stroked his neck but he continued to weave wildly and salivate. As soon as I had got the head collar on and opened his stable door, he barged out and tried to tug me up the lane. The gulping and salivating stopped as quickly as they had begun.

"I'll take him up to the field and see what he's like there," I said.

Alexander immediately settled to graze with his chums on the side of the hill. When the vet arrived, he was munching away and showed her a clean pair of heels when she tried to approach.

"Nothing wrong with him," she declared.

The consensus was that he had bustled angrily round in his box when he saw his friends being led out, snatched a mouthful of haylage and in his anxiety, forgotten to chew it.

Alexander's antics did not stop there. He regularly reached for the long-handled yard brush kept propped up outside his stable, picked it up in his teeth and waved it wildly from side to side in a sweeping motion. He then petulantly flung it to the ground and resumed his extreme weaving.

But he quickly settled at Farfield and we were soon making use of the facilities.

The livery centre has two indoor schools, an outdoor arena and a showjumping paddock, which overlooks the stunning Wharfe Valley. The bigger of the indoor schools is particularly amazing, posher than many competition venues. When Charles showed us round Farfield, on a baking hot day in June 2014, we gazed in awe at the school's airy vastness and expensive soft yellowy surface, the same as that at the London Olympia arena. We could scarcely believe we would soon be riding our horses in it and we still refer to it as 'Posh School.'

Wonderful as all these facilities are, when we began our race training it was the steep, winding track from the stable yard on to the hilltops that proved to be Farfield's most valuable asset. After prolonged downpours, the fields were too wet to use – though they would soon be the focus of our faster work – so we concentrated on riding up and down the stony track. It was ideal for building Alexander's fitness and stamina and we trotted and cantered up it several times on most days.

In our first training session, we walked up the hill, then walked back down. Next we trotted up and walked down. Finally, I asked him to canter up. As we got near to the top he slowed down and seemed ready to go back to a walk. It was getting harder work for him and he thought perhaps he wouldn't bother. But I pushed him on to the top, where we stopped to admire the spectacular views. Alexander was puffing a little but he soon got his breath back. Hard work or not, it seemed to inspire him. He was generally laid back, and even lazy at times, when we rode out. But after walking back down the hill he suddenly burst into a powerful trot and proceeded to trot all the way back to the yard.

I took the opportunity to practise standing up in the stirrups, which I would have to do throughout the race. It was hard work and I struggled to keep my balance, sometimes falling back into the saddle. But towards the end of the trot, I managed to stay upright, resting my hands gently on Alexander's neck. He had already twigged that there was something different going on and seemed happy about it. As I got off him, I noticed there was a glint in his eye. Ian had said Alexander would get livelier. Here were early signs of that and I wondered again if I was doing the right thing by putting him back into racing.

Chapter Eight

Ups and Downs

I remembered only too well the dramas I went through when I first got Alexander fresh off the racecourse in 2010. My thoughts turned back to those troubled times.

Things went well at first. He was surprisingly chilled so I rode him down the lane and braved the cross-country field, where we had our first canter. Feeling confident, I decided to push my luck.

"To hell with it! I might as well find out now if it's going to kill me!" I reasoned.

I pointed Alexander at the hill, sloping steeply up to the top of the field, and asked him to gallop. A sudden surge of power thrust me forward and he was off. In what seemed the blink of an eye, he had gone up the gears. It was as if he was back on the racecourse. We hurtled along, far faster than I had ever been taken before. His long stride ate up the ground. The cool air rushed into my face. And yet, despite the speed, I felt secure. He seemed to glide over the grass, so rhythmic was his movement and so sure were his feet. I eased myself out of the saddle and crouched forward, in a poor imitation of a jockey, peering between his big ears as his red mane flew in the momentum. It felt comfortable and it seemed to give him confidence. He was used to being ridden like that.

We were soon halfway up the hill and Alexander showed

no sign of stopping. An anxious thought suddenly hit me. What if I couldn't pull him up? He could easily clear the boundary fence at the top. Fearing to unsettle him by tugging drastically, I gently eased back the reins. Immediately, his pace slackened. Gradually, he went back down the gears until, neatly inside the perimeter of the field, we came to a bouncy stop. The brakes had worked perfectly. We stood at the top of the hill, Alexander puffing slightly from his exertions. He shook his head in appreciation of the exciting gallop.

But not everything went so smoothly. Alexander would hide at the back of his stable, peeping out at us from beneath his orange fringe. He seemed frightened about what the outside world might have to offer.

"It's plotting to kill us," Jenny would say, deeply suspicious of the new arrival lurking monster-like within.

When he came in from the field, Alexander refused to go near the wash area slats to have the mud cleaned off his legs. Nor would he go on the horse walker. I could see worry, fear and uncertainty in his eyes. He needed someone he could trust and love; someone who would trust and love him in return. The last thing he needed was someone to fight with him. Instead of forcing him on to the slats or the walker, I tried gentle encouragement and kind words. And if he had to have dirty legs for a while, then so be it.

I spent time with him every day, brushing him and talking to him. We watched other horses being washed down or revolving on the walker, and I quietly explained to him what was happening and reassured him that nothing nasty would befall him. He stood with me, taking it all in, and I could see the fear starting to fade from his eyes. And then, a week or so into the process, he walked on to the slats with me and we stood together, looking at the water gushing down below. It was a magical moment. For the first time, I felt there was some sort of union between us.

The next day I took him to the horse walker. I opened the metal door with one hand, holding him by his lead rope with the other. The contraption was empty and motionless. The weather was kind, with no wind or rain.

"Do you want a closer look?" I said, and we moved forward on to the shallow step leading into the walker. Alexander stood, his long nose actually inside it. This was as near as we had got. I felt the opportunity was there. I clicked my tongue in encouragement, said quietly: "Come on, then," and, without tugging, put some gentle pressure on the lead rope. I felt him relax his body and he began to move. Suddenly, we were standing in one of the walker's compartments.

"Good boy, good boy," I praised, patting and stroking his neck.

His body language suggested an uncertain acceptance of the situation. He was starting to trust me, but he needed to trust me a bit more.

"Close the door," I said to Jenny.

"What?" The tone of her voice and her look of disbelief told me she was unhappy with what I was planning. But my mind was made up.

"Close the door," I repeated firmly.

It clanged into place, leaving Alexander and me enclosed inside.

"Turn it on. Keep it at a slow speed," I instructed.

Jenny did as I asked. The walker began to move. I clicked my tongue again and told Alexander to walk on. Linked together by the lead rope, like an umbilical cord, we shuffled forward and began slowly revolving.

This was not a concept taken from any health and safety manual. In fact, it flew in the face of common sense. I was taking a big risk. The metal sides of the walker, and the compartment dividers, were eight feet high. There was no way out, for the horse or for me. I was trapped. If Alexander panicked and reared or kicked out in that confined space, I could be seriously injured. And no one could get to me quickly or easily. But I was prepared to take the risk. Alexander needed me and I was going to be there for him. If I could get him over his walker phobia it would be a massive stride forward. We walked two circuits together, then Jenny stopped the machine and I emerged. I had achieved my aim. Alexander was now settled and I stood outside, proudly watching as he walked round on his own. After half a dozen circuits, we switched off the walker and I led him back to his stable. He looked pleased with himself. I was delighted. I had put my faith in him and he had rewarded me with his trust.

A few days later, I jumped him for the first time, at our favourite cross-country training ground, Craven Country Ride. When Alexander caught sight of the rolling fields, dotted with rustic jumps, he seemed to grow. There was an anticipation and a simmering excitement about him. He began sweating and jogging when we reached the first line of flagged fences. He was itching to run but he was polite enough to wait for me, and when I released him, I was in control of the canter, steering him well clear of the fences and pulling up safely at the end of the field.

The next meadow offered a small but inviting log. Alexander's eyes were on stalks and he tugged at the reins. Just as eager, I turned towards the log and let him go. He bounded towards the fence and I sat quietly, squeezing my lower legs around him and thrusting my heels down to keep my balance. He sprang over the 18-inch jump, giving it at least the same height in clearance, and excitedly cantered up a slope on the other side.

We carried on round the course, walking and trotting,

having the occasional controlled canter and jumping a few small and simple obstacles.

Alexander's behaviour was impressive until we paused for homemade cake and fruit punch, a traditional treat served up to the riders halfway round the trail. Alexander was enjoying himself so much he did not want to stop. Our five minute break became an ordeal for everyone else as he refused to stand still. I just about managed to drink the contents of my little plastic cup but my daughter Sophie, who was riding Daniel, had no such luck. My impatient steed suddenly reversed at speed, barging into an indignant Daniel and squashing him against a gate. Sophie's complimentary fruit punch was spilled everywhere.

Alexander could be a frightening sight in those early days. A few weeks after he arrived, we took him to Skipton Horse Trials for a saddle fitting by a local firm with a trade stand at the event. The crowds and the blaring commentary must have convinced Alexander he was back at the races. His long neck grew alarmingly as he craned it out of the side door of the trailer. His eyes rolled, his nostrils flared and he neighed shudderingly and repeatedly while booting the inside of the trailer. We sought help from local event rider David Elms to hang on to Alexander's head collar while the saddle fitting took place.

David was assisting me at the time by riding Alexander in the outdoor arena at our yard. The thoroughbred had probably never been schooled before and it was hard work, so he wasn't very keen. One day the pair had a terrible fall-out. David is a strong rider and used to getting his own way. But the young Alexander was stubborn and backward thinking, and wanted to take the easy option. The more David tried to get Alexander to work properly, the more frustrated and angry the horse became. He started to roll his eyes wildly. He was simmering and the explosion was not long in coming. Alexander started to throw his head from side to side, then he shook his whole body and began to rear. It was clear he was trying to bring the schooling to an end by removing David, who was having none of it. It takes a lot to dislodge him, and his failure to do so made Alexander even more angry. The angrier he got, the more determined David became.

I watched from outside the school as the battle grew more intense. It was enthralling and terrifying at the same time. I wondered how I would have coped, but quickly put the uncomfortable thought out of my head.

At last, the disagreement came to an end. Now tired, Alexander admitted defeat, but not before he had deliberately rammed David into the boundary fence, leaving him bruised and sore.

The incident brought home to me that falling out with Alexander was to be avoided. The best way for me to ride him was quietly but positively. I had to ignore his occasional tantrums and keep moving him forward. I was, however, forced to take firm and decisive action when Alexander caught sight of an old commentary box brought out of retirement for a horse event the yard was hosting. David was walking with us for a lesson in the showjumping field when Alexander began reversing back down the lane. David told me to act. If Alexander was allowed to get away with it, it would create huge problems for the future. I managed to stop him. Slowly, with determination and a strong leg, I inched him forward until the commentary box came back into view. Alexander was still trying to wriggle out of it, but I held him in position and with a final squeeze of my legs, I got him into the field. It was a significant victory that proved both to myself, and to Alexander, that if there was a battle to be had, it was possible for me to win it.

It was several weeks before I had my first fall from

Alexander. By now it was midsummer and, worried that my ex-racer was getting a little on the sleepy side during the warm June days, I decided to feed him Baby Horse's leftover oats. It was not my smartest decision. While oats are ideal for giving a bit of vim to a lazy, lumbering chap like Baby, they are like rocket fuel to a fit thoroughbred. We had sailed over a small fence in the cross-country field when Alexander bucked, twisted in the air and bucked again. I hit the ground hard and bounced, while Alexander hurtled riderless up the meadow. It was far different from tumbling off Daniel. I had further to fall from the tall thoroughbred, and his speed, power and athleticism meant I was launched with much greater velocity. It happened so quickly I had little chance to even think about it, let alone do anything to stop it. I stayed down for a few seconds, slightly stunned, then got to my feet. My hat silk and whip had been hurled yards away, but apart from bruises and a minor finger injury, I was unscathed and undaunted.

Over the next couple of years, the falls came thick and fast; my eagerness to push myself in the jumping stakes, and Alexander's temperamental mood swings, leading too often to my downfall. But I kept getting back on and soon got a reputation for persistence in the face of adversity. After one particularly eventful day at Craven Country Ride, an amazed onlooker commented: "That man on the chestnut's a resilient bugger. It's already come past twice without him!"

I came a right cropper one morning after deciding to tackle a new fence at the bottom of the cross-country meadow. Alexander flew it effortlessly but as he landed, he shot off to the right and began to turn himself inside out. I slammed into the hard ground with my left knee.

Jenny, who was riding with me, said Alexander had twisted so high in the air, with all four legs off the ground, that all she could see was the underneath of his ginger tummy.

As I lay prone, she feared I was really seriously hurt and went to get help. I told her I was all right but I wasn't convinced and I lay there for a full five minutes until the pain in my knee began to subside. When I did move, the best I could manage was to spin sideways on the ground. My knee seemed to be bending, which was good news, but it had already swollen to twice its normal size and there was a hole in my jodhpurs through which protruded bloody flesh.

Carefully, I sat up and then, with an effort, got to my feet. The knee was still throbbing but I could put weight on it. It seemed I had been fortunate.

As I stood there on my own it looked an awful long way to the top of the hill. I set off at a steady hobble and was relieved to be able to do so. Moving the knee helped and the further I limped the freer it got. But I was still in considerable pain. When friends at the yard saw me limping about in my ripped, bloodied and grass-stained jodhpurs they urged me to go to hospital for a check up. But I knew that, though badly bumped, bruised and scraped, I was not seriously injured. What I needed was a drink. The jodhpurs were in danger of sticking to the wound so I cut the knee out of them and dragged myself to the pub for a lager and a roast beef Sunday lunch. Diners turned in consternation as I hobbled to a sunny, outdoor table. I was doing nothing to banish the fears of many parents with pony mad offspring that horse riding is a highly dangerous pursuit!

Some of my falls had slapstick elements to them, like the time I came off while indoor showjumping. The first fence on the course was quite wide. It was to be jumped towards the perimeter wall, with a left turn to the second fence. Alexander's ears were pricked in excitement and he stood off the fence and took a great leap. We sailed through the air, but his huge jump took us perilously close to the wall. Before I could react, he shied violently to the right to avoid it. I kept going straight ahead, flew into the wall and bounced off it. I was shaken but suffered only bruising to my hand, wrist and lower back, and a degree of embarrassment. I was helped from the arena and sat at a table in the café with a bag of frozen peas on my hand to prevent it swelling. As I left, I managed to spill most of the peas on the floor. A small boy watched fascinated as I tried to pick them up while they bounced and rolled around ridiculously.

The injuries I suffered in my falls were mostly minor, but I had to visit the accident and emergency department after Alexander again bucked me off spectacularly in the cross-country field. We set off from the bottom of the hill but Alexander had galloped only two or three strides when he put his head between his knees. When he bucks he doesn't stop at one. And they tend to be big. I was launched and my horse pelted up the hill on his own.

I gingerly got up but I could barely put one foot in front of the other because of the pain and stiffness. I couldn't pinpoint where it hurt most but I had a terrible aching in my lower back and groin area.

An ambulance took me to Airedale General Hospital where I was put in a wheelchair and trundled ignominiously into A & E. When Jenny and Sophie arrived, they couldn't find me. Then they spotted a pair of socked feet sticking out from behind a wall. They went round the corner and found me hunched crossly in the wheelchair. It was an amusing sight, though I wasn't finding the experience funny. I felt even less like smiling when I was examined by the doctor.

"I'm sending you for X-rays," she said. "There's a possibility you have fractured your pelvis."

I hadn't expected anything as serious as that. But the results of the X-rays brought good news. There was no fracture of the pelvis, or anything else. My injury turned out to be more embarrassing than serious. I had stretched the ligament between the pelvic and pubic bones, resulting in everything turning a deep shade of purple! It took time to heal and I was out of the saddle for five weeks.

That fall happened two days before we were due to go to our first horse camp at Somerford Park in Cheshire. The equestrian centre hosts major eventing and dressage competitions, as well as regular horse camps where you are taught showjumping and cross-country by professional riders. The three-day camps are a learning curve, a real challenge to horse and jockey, and you are pushed hard by the instructors.

Seven months later, we made it to Somerford but I was to suffer another dramatic fall there that taught me much about my relationship with Alexander.

As part of my preparations for the camp, I had a cross-country lesson at Craven Country Ride with former international event rider Claire Fitzmaurice. She encouraged me to be in charge of the partnership and had us jumping smaller fences in a steady manner. Alexander had to go at the pace I wanted him to, when I wanted it. Everything went well until almost the end of the lesson. We were given a line of four uphill fences to jump, still not very big. We popped over the first and then Alexander took off. We hurdled the second at a gallop, ignored the last two and hurtled to the top of the hill, where I managed to pull him up.

Claire was furious.

"That was a disgrace. Do it again, properly," she ordered, shouting: "You shouldn't have a fucking racehorse if you can't fucking stop it!"

The first evening at Somerford is a night of excited anticipation. Everyone is psyching themselves up for the following day, wondering what group they will be in and which teacher they will get. The drink flows steadily but no one is late to bed.

The second evening is a highlight. That is when the professional photographer turns up, armed with individual packs of action shots from that day's cross-country and showjumping sessions. There is great excitement at the arrival of the picture lady. There are squeals of delight and gasps of admiration as everyone's photos are passed around the clubhouse. The snaps capture special moments and are treasured and gazed at for many years to come.

The weather was glorious for our Somerford debut. It was the only hot week of the summer and I rode in a T-shirt and body protector.

Showjumping was first up. It should have been a good way to build our confidence, but the session was disappointing. Somerford can be daunting and I was a bundle of nerves. My riding technique went out of the window as my confidence evaporated. Alexander, realising all was not well up top, began to worry. The pair of us were fretting and so not working as a team. We had terrible trouble at a tight turn into a double and kept getting it all wrong. My balance in the saddle was not as it should be, which unbalanced my horse, and we knocked down a lot of poles.

I was down in the dumps over lunch, assessing what had gone wrong, but I came out for the afternoon cross-country session with my confidence restored. I felt that this was our best chance of success and I thought Alexander would enjoy it more. He picked up on my mood and suddenly the team was back. Somerford is about being pushed, and we were. We rose to the challenge, jumping three-foot-high courses, including logs, tyres, brush fences, a house and, a little reluctantly, a three-foot-wide open ditch.

Dinner tasted better that evening for our performance and we were raring to go the next morning when we went back out on the cross-country course. My instructor Bianca Bairstow was pleased with our efforts the previous day. Now it was time to push on.

We set off in fine style around another three-foot course - tyres, a rail fence, two logs, a brush fence and then the house, which we flew. The open ditch was the final obstacle to clear. We approached it steadily, but at the last moment Alexander ducked it. I came off him but landed on my feet. It was my first fall at Somerford, and a harmless one. My second one would be less so.

I got back on and Bianca told me to approach again. We jumped the house, but again Alexander stopped at the ditch. I kept him at the edge as he dug his toes in, not letting him turn away. He still refused to jump it, clearly worried by the big open gap. It became a battle of wills and I had to win it. I gave him a couple of slaps down the shoulder with the whip, held him in position and kept squeezing him with my leg. And then I felt his back end begin to coil and I knew he was going to jump. Suddenly, from a standstill, Alexander launched himself skywards. The leap was huge and there was no way I could sit it. I flew through the air and landed heavily. Dry weather meant that the sandy ground around the jumps had become very hard, making the fall a real boneshaker. I bashed my knee, foot and hand and ripped a hole in my jodhpurs, from which blood seeped.

As I lay down to recover, Alexander went galloping back to the stables, bucking spectacularly.

I was shaken up but not badly hurt. Jenny wanted me to quit for the day but I knew I had to get back on. I sat quietly for ten minutes, remounted and rejoined the group. To regain my confidence, Bianca asked me to jump a two-foot roll top, a fairly standard and simple jump. But as I turned Alexander into it, something was wrong and he ducked out to the left. Then he refused it again.

I knew the problem was in my head. My confidence had disappeared and taken Alexander's with it. For the first time as a rider, my nerve - my bottle - had gone. I just hadn't been able to ride Alexander into the fence. I was scared. It was a big thing to have to admit to myself. But that was it, in a word. Scared.

And because I was scared, so was Alexander. That told me he wasn't the big, fearless steeplechaser-cum-cross-country horse I had thought he was. In fact, he was more fragile and fearful than I could have imagined. It was becoming clear to me why he had failed on the racecourse. He might have all the physical attributes, but he didn't have the bottle on his own. He had to get it from his rider. And he had come to rely massively on me. If I was confident and positive, so was he. But the moment I wavered, he went to pieces. He needed me to give him the courage and then he could take on pretty much anything.

I had gone to Somerford to find out what sort of competitive team we could be. I had learned some very interesting lessons about our relationship. It ran deeper than I had realised and our dependence on each other was startling. If we gave each other the belief, there might be nothing we couldn't achieve. But it was beginning to dawn on me that we had our limits.

Days after getting back from my ill-fated trip to Somerford, I began the task of rebuilding my shattered confidence. David Elms volunteered his help and we set off to Craven Country Ride. I still had faith in my horse and I knew David was the ideal person to get me back on track.

We trotted round to warm up and then David asked me to ride into a tiny one-foot log. As we approached the little log I got the same sickly feeling of fear as when I tried to jump the roll top after my fall at Somerford. Alexander instantly picked up on it. He veered away and I let him dance over the edge of the obstacle.

I had bottled it again. If I couldn't jump that, what hope was there for anything bigger?

David let rip at me.

"That was just rubbish," he barked.

"Shorten your reins, get your leg on him and make him jump it properly."

As we came in again, David's voice rang out: "Leg on and ride him!"

I did as I was told. I felt Alexander twitch to the right. David was still shouting instructions. I squeezed harder with my leg and Alexander straightened up and jumped the little log.

"That's better," shouted David.

"Keep going. Bring him round and do it again, just the same."

So I did. And we jumped it again, more fluently.

Suddenly, I felt as if a great weight had been lifted from my shoulders. I thought to myself: "Yes, you can do this."

We moved to another log, a bit bigger and more gnarled. I kept my leg on and this time Alexander broke into a canter. I kept squeezing and we soared over the bigger log.

"Much, much better," declared David.

Next we jumped a little course; the two logs followed by a bigger rail fence. We were fluent and positive. The confidence was beginning to flow back into both of us. The rebuilding process had begun.

David had been tough on me but it was exactly what I needed to make me face up to what I had to do. And it had worked.

After that, we tackled the Multi Bank, the water complex, more logs and a line of jumps, including a brush fence.

Satisfied, David said we could finish with a course of our own selection in the last field. I picked a brush fence on top of yellow pipes for our final flourish. I fancied the look of it, but as we approached the jump, it seemed to grow in size. My negative thoughts went straight down the reins. Feeling my uncertainty, Alexander ducked out to the left. I had given myself a major problem. We had spent the last hour putting our confidence back together. Now our fragility had brought it crashing down again.

I knew I had no alternative but to jump the fence. If I accepted defeat it would undo everything we had achieved in the day. I had to be brave enough to take it on and to give Alexander the courage to do it. I rode in positively. I felt Alexander's doubts but I over-ruled them with my determination. He sprang and we were over. I kept him cantering round and approached the big brush again. This time Alexander was more confident. He stood off the fence and gave it some daylight as we went over. It was a very big jump for a novice like me but I kept my leg in the right place and was still rock solid in the saddle as we landed. I felt a rush of emotions - exhilaration, pride and relief.

David strode up.

"When I said you could jump anything, I didn't think it was necessary to tell you not to jump the biggest fence in the field."

His voice was stern but there was a twinkle in his eye.

I had made the wrong decision in my choice of fence but I had put it right with my riding.

I asked David how high the fence was. He stood next to it and announced: "Between 3ft 3ins and 3ft 6ins."

It was the highest I had ever jumped Alexander.

Chapter Nine

The Gateway Of Doom

While my gung-ho attitude to riding my ex-racehorse was mostly to blame for my accidents, my worst fall happened during a fun dressage contest at our yard on a sunny Sunday in February 2013. It left me with far more serious injuries and called into question the whole future of my relationship with Alexander.

It was supposed to be an informal and gentle introduction to a new season of competition. Alexander looked a picture. Jenny had bathed him, brushed his thick red tail, neatly plaited his orange mane and oiled his hooves. She was thrilled to receive the trophy for Best Turned Out Horse.

Jenny was keen to watch my dressage test, but she had to head for Bradford for her shift at the Telegraph & Argus. She left me walking calmly round the sunlit arena, waiting to start.

"Cheer me up at work with a text to say you've won a rosette," she called across the car park.

I felt confident we would do well. With only six rivals, maybe we could even win.

"Won't be long now, lad," I said reassuringly to Alexander. I had warmed him up and was ready to start as soon as two other riders had finished their preparations and left the arena. One cantered past us and I automatically stretched out my hand to soothingly stroke Alexander's neck. But he was perfectly calm and continued to stroll forward nonchalantly. I was riding him on a loose rein to keep him relaxed. Who could possibly have guessed, as I walked round the arena in the sunshine, that I was seconds from disaster?

I saw one of the riders cantering towards us and I turned Alexander on to the inside line and began to walk him across the centre of the school. As the rider came past behind us, I felt a sudden surge of power; a bunching of muscle. In an instant, Alexander had accelerated from a walk to a flat-out, panicked gallop. I had no time to react and was immediately out of control. He swept round at full pelt in a sharp, right-handed arc. I was nearly thrown off the side of him but somehow managed to cling on. Then I saw the arena fence and wooden gate rushing up to meet us. Into my whirling brain came the certain knowledge of crunching bone. I felt a sickening thud as my body was slammed into the solid gatepost, and saw the blurred faces of the horrified spectators. Then I was catapulted into the air.

I lay outside the arena with my arms and legs splayed and sand in my mouth. I was conscious, but in a complete daze. All I knew was that I was alive. That was a good start. Then I became aware of the pain. It confirmed that I was indeed alive. It was intense and coming from two places, around the left hip or pelvis, and a more agonising pain from the rib area in my lower back on the same side. More frighteningly, I was having trouble breathing. I could only snatch short, sharp gasps of air. I knew I had to keep calm, but I was too stunned to panic.

I was vaguely aware of someone asking if I could move my arms and legs, and I was relieved to find that I could feebly wave them. Everything was hazy, as if I was looking in on something that was happening to somebody else. It was the haze of pain. Nothing else registered.

I began spitting sand out of my mouth. It reminded me I

was wearing my hat, and I managed to unhook it and lift it off. I tried to take off my riding gloves, and somebody helped. I wanted to ask if Alexander was all right, but I didn't have the breath to get the words out. The pain was everything. I tried to wriggle away from it, but there was no escape. Someone was telling me not to move. And then I became aware of paramedics at my side, checking me over.

After a few minutes, one of them asked: "Do you feel able to get up?"

"No, but I'll do it," and with them firmly holding on to me, I managed.

One painful step at a time, a paramedic on either side of me, I shuffled the few feet to the back of the ambulance and got in. The younger paramedic stayed with me and carefully helped me to lie down on my back on the stretcher. He covered me with blankets and the ambulance set off to hospital, my second visit to Airedale General.

The young paramedic was both cheerful and philosophical.

"You have a choice of three types of pain relief. But you have to choose. I can't do it for you."

Only two of the options registered in my pain-numbed brain, paracetamol and morphine. I recalled Jenny telling me once how wonderful the latter had been when she was in hospital.

"Morphine?" I suggested.

The young paramedic winked. "That's the one."

Within seconds of the injection, a comforting warmth began to flow through me and the pain was dulled. My breathing, which had been laboured, became easier. I began to notice my surroundings. Just above my head was a clock. It told me it was five past two in the afternoon.

"Is that helping?" asked the young man.

I smiled for the first time. "It feels rather good."

A few minutes later he gave me a second shot.

"Don't tell anyone I've filled you full of smack!" he grinned.

At the hospital, I had to wait on my stretcher in a corridor. It was a typically busy Sunday afternoon. The paramedics stayed with me. They were a comfort. They and the morphine.

When a cubicle became free, the ambulance crew left me. But Jenny appeared soon after. She had brought two of my children, Sophie and Ben.

"How's Alexander? Is he hurt?" I asked anxiously, looking up at their pale and troubled faces.

"Don't worry, he's fine," Jenny said. "His nose was bleeding and he has minor cuts to his front legs and chest but they have been cleaned up and he's resting in his stable."

It looked like being a long wait at the hospital, and when my family had to leave I was still on my trolley in the cubicle. Eventually, I went for X-rays and was then trundled on to a small and quiet surgical ward. The following day a CT scan revealed the extent of my injuries – three broken ribs, a cracked pelvis and a punctured lung, which had been responsible for my breathing difficulties. The lung would quickly re-inflate and the bones would mend themselves, but it would take two to three months.

"You're going to have to be patient. It won't be quick," warned the orthopaedic surgeon.

I was in hospital for three days. I wore green stockings to prevent thrombosis and a patterned hospital gown that gaped at the back, drawing gasps of pity from fellow patients at the massive area of black bruising on my hips, lower back and legs.

The accident had happened less than three years after Alexander came into my life. Many critics were now saying it was time I got rid of him, for my own safety. I disagreed. As I lay in my hospital bed, I reflected on what had happened and concluded that my horse was completely blameless.

Witnesses described how he shot off 'as if he had been stung' and some said he had been accidentally flicked on his bottom by the other rider's long schooling whip. Extra care should be taken around a thoroughbred like Alexander, who has known the adrenaline rush of the racecourse. He had clearly reacted to the whip and panicked.

I was surprised to find that Alexander had a supporter in Ian Conroy, never the biggest fan of my horse.

"It was just a freak accident," Ian said. "You have to remember that horse has had his backside whipped plenty of times in the past. He must have thought he was in for some more and ran off in panic."

However, I was concerned that three years of painstaking work to build Alexander's confidence and form a partnership with him had been destroyed by one rash moment. But we had given our hearts to each other and that would serve us well in rebuilding the bridges.

Two weeks after my accident, I was reunited with Alexander when Jenny took me to the stables. I was excited by the prospect. Sitting at home, I had missed him terribly. He is not a demonstrative horse. I didn't expect him to neigh with delight when he saw me, but it didn't stop me from hoping. Nor did it prevent me from being disappointed when he stayed silent. I called his name as I hobbled across the yard towards his stable. He did not move forward to greet me, but stood stock still, eyeing me quizzically.

"It's me, Dad," I said at the stable door.

Alexander continued to stare at me, his big ears moving back and forth. He seemed to be trying to work out what I was doing there, as if he had not expected me back. I went into his stable and he let me stroke him and chatter away, but he remained suspicious. Clearly, his security had taken a knock.

The next time I went to see him he was more relaxed and seemed happy that things were getting back to normal. He poked gently for mints with his long nose and showed an interest in what I was doing.

At first, I could hardly get about at all. I was under doctor's orders to stay at home and rest so that my bones could knit. The best bet for a speedy recovery was to sit in my armchair, under my tartan rug, and do nothing. As the weeks passed I was no longer in pain, but I still walked with a limp. I had to stick to short distances and be careful not to twist or stretch. The healing process was very slow. I was bored, lonely and down. My days were broken up only by a fifty yard stroll to the Co-op to buy tea.

As I sat for long hours in my chair through those dreary days of recovery, it crossed my mind that I would never ride Alexander again after such a crashing fall.

At the weekends, Jenny took me to the yard for short visits. The bitter cold meant I couldn't hang around for long, but it was wonderful to see Alexander and spend time with him. I was able to carefully skip him out and put extra straw down for him. I felt he knew Dad still cared, even if he wasn't around all the time. I drew comfort and hope from the strength of our relationship during those visits. Alexander seemed to like me being there, brushing him, fastening his rug, or just relaxing together. Often he would gaze at me with his big, light brown eyes. I was never quite certain what lay behind them, but I got an impression of concern, and understanding, and, dare I say, love. The feelings were mutual.

Jenny baked a cake for Alexander's ninth birthday. It was probably a good job I wasn't able to ride him as it was made of energy-giving Quaker Oats, treacle and honey, and topped with apples and carrots. It was on a decorated plate in a carrier bag and Alexander sniffed it out straight away. He tried to get his nose in the bag and then peered into the feed room, ears pricked, as I cut a thick slice for him.

Gradually, I was able to do more. I began to drive the short journey to the yard and I was able to stay longer and do a few more jobs. I filled my first haynet in weeks and wheeled it in a barrow to the stable; washed the horses' supper bowls and put Alexander's saddle away.

Then I managed to carefully muck out the stables, lift a straw bale and empty full wheelbarrows. After six weeks off, I returned to work, successfully driving in with just a couple of slight twinges to my ribs when changing gear.

It was April when I got back on Alexander and, at last, there were real signs of spring after the long and bitter winter. The weather was mild and sunny, and although ribbons of snow still clung to the hillsides, daffodils, dandelions and celandines carpeted the grass verges.

I planned to start riding again at the end of the month, around ten weeks after my fall. The prospect filled me with excitement, but I was also nervous about how he might react. The closeness I felt to Alexander would help when I rode him again, but with the big day getting near I knew it was equally important to be in control, so when he nipped my arm in an over-enthusiastic quest for mints, he got a smack. Usually, he anticipates a chastisement and sways out of range, like an equine version of Muhammad Ali, but this time I got him. The next day it was clear he had learned his lesson. His manners were perfect. He didn't even nudge for a mint, but just looked hopeful, and I rewarded him.

A few days later I tied Alexander up on the edge of the wash slats while I sat nearby and got myself ready to ride. As I put on my riding boots I became aware of Alexander looking over at me. I glanced up. He watched my every move as I fastened my riding chaps around my lower legs. When I put on my hat, his eyes seemed to widen and his ears waggled backward and forward – just like the first time he saw me after the accident. I thought I could detect concern in his eye. Jenny tacked him up. He was chilled but still had a slightly wondrous expression.

"Don't worry," I said. "Dad's fine."

Jenny led him to the big stone mounting block and held him as I gathered the reins in my left hand and placed my right hand on the back of the saddle. He stood perfectly still as I swung my leg across his back and sat astride him. There had been no physical difficulty getting back on, but my heart was racing. I nudged Alexander forward and we took our first few steps over the canal bridge and along the lane. As we rode away, someone commented: "I don't know which of you has got the biggest smile!"

After two months out of the saddle, I had forgotten what it was like to ride. More than that, I had forgotten what it was like to ride a thoroughbred. When I first rode Alexander, I was enthralled by his bounce, sway and swagger. Now I was getting that feeling again. His quality came to me afresh, and I was again enthralled.

I wasn't going to be ambitious on the first ride. We simply pottered along for a short distance, turned round and trundled back again. Alexander was quiet and relaxed, as if he knew this was a test for me and wanted to help put me at ease.

"Isn't this great?" I said, patting his neck. He twitched his ears and snorted, and seemed to agree.

When we were nearly back at the yard I suddenly found the pelvic sway that makes it easier to ride a thoroughbred. For a few strides we hit a rhythm and Alexander noticeably moved quicker and better.

Jenny dashed to fetch her phone to get a photograph of me back on board. She expected me to follow her on to the yard, but I had other ideas. I needed to lay my ghost. I had to prove that my terrible accident was just that. I had to ride in the school again. And I had to do it now. I sneaked round the corner. The outdoor arena was empty. Here was my chance. Alexander hesitated slightly as I rode him towards the open gate, the one I had hurtled over.

"It's all right, lad. We'll just pop in for a minute," I said softly.

And then we were through the gate and in the school. Alexander was calm and unfazed.

"We're here now, let's get on with it," I thought.

I asked for a trot. There was a moment of reluctance, as though Alexander didn't want anything to go wrong. And then he trotted. It felt a little unnatural, as if I wasn't quite with him. But we were trotting. We circled the arena and then went out of the gate and walked back to the yard. I felt both relief and a sense of achievement. It would take a few more rides to get back into the swing of it, and my nerve was bound to be tested.

But it was a case of so far so good.

The Gateway of Doom

Chapter Ten

Our First Win

I knew that competing again on Alexander after fracturing my ribs and pelvis was going to be mentally tough. It was one thing to walk down the lane and trot round the school, but quite another to jump him in a competition. I was unsure how I would cope, but it was clear that I would have to. Competing was important to me. It was the reason I had got Alexander, to have a horse who could run and jump at speed and give me the chance of winning.

The first time I competed on Alexander was at a one-day event at Richmond Equestrian Centre, in North Yorkshire, two years earlier. It involved a simple walk and trot dressage test, showjumping and a rustic working hunter course. The jumping phases were over two-foot fences, less than half the height Alexander had been used to leaping when racing, but big enough for me. We practised hard for our big day. Alexander was still unenthusiastic about schooling but he was starting to accept that it had to be done. The same could be said of me. Although the cross-country phase was the exciting bit, no matter how good our jumping was we wouldn't have a chance of any prizes if our dressage test was poor.

Ex-racehorses can find showjumping difficult but Alexander seemed to have a natural talent for it. Some horses are unnerved by brightly coloured showjumps, or garishly designed 'fillers,' placed underneath the poles as an added difficulty. Alexander was untroubled. Whatever the fence, he came bouncing in and sprang over it without a second glance, and then looked for the next one. His enthusiasm helped me. I had always considered myself better suited to cross-country riding, where bravery counts more than style, and I had felt too lacking in technique to be a successful showjumper. But now I had a horse that was taking me round, without me having to kick, and I was able to relax more.

I was nervous as I sat astride my edgy thoroughbred at Richmond. Alexander looked impressive with his plaited mane and leggy muscular frame. I was wearing my smart black showjumping jacket, gold fox's head stock pin and white dressage gloves. I may have looked the part but I didn't feel it.

The dressage was indoors. We pranced from the wagon park to the warm-up arena. It was big, which was a bonus. The more room we had for manoeuvre, the better. There were only a couple of horse and rider combinations warming up when we entered the collecting ring but it was enough to make Alexander twitchy. He felt like a coiled spring as we walked and trotted round and I concentrated on keeping the lid on him by relaxing my hands, moving him forward and talking quietly to him. He tugged his head around but I had control.

All too soon, it was time to enter the main arena. The dressage was the part I was least looking forward to. It was only the second test I had ever ridden. Even though it was as simple as they come, I was worried I would not remember it, or that we would make a mess of it. But for a first attempt it went surprisingly well. We made no mistakes and I was delighted with our mark of 57.82 per cent. The judge's comments were: "A very nice horse with good paces, just a little tense today. Calmly ridden."

Alexander went into a wonderful bouncy canter for our showjumping round. We would have had a clear round had I not lost my way after the first fence and been forced to circle, costing us four faults.

He was equally keen in the working hunter phase, towing me into the fences, but carelessly knocking off a couple of poles with his front legs.

We finished with 12 jumping penalties to add to our dressage score. There were only three in our class but I was happy to be a close and competitive third and to win a yellow rosette.

Our first competition after my dressage accident would be a challenge so I wanted it to be at a place where I felt comfortable and had enjoyed some success.

Camp Hill in North Yorkshire was the obvious choice. It is my favourite event venue and has given me so much belief as a rider over the years. It is run by professional eventer Eleanor Mercer and is in the heart of an idyllic country estate. From May to September, Camp Hill hosts a series of monthly cross-country competitions, at heights from 50cms to 80cms. The fences are not over-facing but the courses are technically challenging. It is a great place for inexperienced or nervous riders and horses to gain confidence.

Points are awarded each month to the top ten competitors and added together to produce winners of each class at the end of the season. In 2012, we had finished third in the 50cms series. The aim in 2013 had been to step up to the 65cms class. That now seemed a big ask.

My preparations began with a riding lesson, during which I cantered Alexander for the first time since our accident. As I performed figures of eight and walk to canter transitions, the confidence started to flow. I was knackered by the end of the lesson, but a great weight had been lifted from me emotionally. I had taken a big step forward.

Two weeks later, I had a second lesson. It was in the showjumping field and we got to tackle a little course of four fences, about two feet high. I was nervous but I was helped by Alexander. He was calm and controlled, and very measured at his jumps. Nothing to alarm or unbalance me. We were working for each other. The close bond we had formed after the accident, in and around his stable, was paying off. The nerves were still there, especially when I did something I hadn't done since I was injured. But one by one, I was ticking the boxes.

It was less than a fortnight to Camp Hill and Alexander was full of himself and ready for action. He looked fit and had filled out. His back end was bigger and his muscles were firm. Out in the field he was bursting with energy, racing around flat out, bucking wildly and rearing up over other horses in his exuberance.

One day I plucked up the courage to have some jumping practice in the cross-country field. I selected a small log near the bottom gate. It was a harmless little obstacle we had jumped many times but as we cantered towards it, it began to take on the appearance of Becher's Brook. But Alexander jumped it calmly and confidently and pulled up for me immediately afterwards.

"Thanks, lad," I said, patting him.

Then we tackled the bank. I wasn't going to go off the end of it, even though I had done so many times before. But it would be a start if we went across it, where the drop was smaller. Alexander flew up on to the bank and sprang athletically off the other side. I was a bit wobbly on landing.

"Could have done with being sat further back," I thought. But I was safe, and again Alexander pulled up. I patted his neck once more.

"That's enough for today, lad. Thanks again."

So that was another box ticked. And Alexander had helped me to do it. My respect and affection for him had just grown a bit more. It seemed that he was feeling the same. He had begun to neigh when I arrived at the yard, and to weave with excitement.

"It's really touching,"said Jenny. "He never neighs for anyone else, but he bellows a greeting when he sees you."

Alexander's summer coat had come through. Standing tall, he was a splendid and heart-stopping sight as he looked across from the top of his summer meadow, over the Dales to Malham Cove and beyond. With his big ears pricked and his flame-coloured mane flowing in the evening breeze, he could have been a wild stallion surveying his domain. Alexander is a fine example of the British thoroughbred, long-limbed and slender-necked. His long, narrow head, with its crooked white blaze, was now carried with a supreme confidence. His tail, red as a fox's brush, billowed out behind him. His coat glowed like copper in the late spring sun, the veins standing out under his delicate skin. To me, he was the most beautiful horse in the world.

Camp Hill was just as we remembered it. As we pulled through the entrance gates, we saw rolling meadows covered in wild flowers and the ancient manor house overlooking the beautiful rural scene.

We found a parking spot next to the warm-up field. As we opened the side door of the trailer, Alexander's long orange neck snaked out and he peered round enthusiastically at the practice fences. He neighed loudly as he saw other horses being ridden around.

"Are you glad we've come?"I asked.

Alexander snorted in appreciation and craned his neck

even further in the direction of the fences.

It was a beautiful day, fine and sunny but with a refreshing breeze. Perfect conditions. Jenny brought Alexander out of the trailer and at once he was nibbling at the grass.

"Cool customer," I thought, pleased.

I left him with Jenny while I walked the 50cms course. It was effectively a big loop. The fences were familiar friends from the previous year. The little course shouldn't present us with any problems, unless we created them for ourselves. But seeing Alexander nonchalantly munching at the grass made me feel calmer. There was no reason why we shouldn't jump clear and try to get near the optimum time. Jenny was keen for us to get a rosette, but the sun had brought everybody out. There were more than forty competitors in the class. Rosettes went to tenth.

I rolled up the sleeves of my navy blue and mustard-coloured cross-country shirt to above the elbows. It is a tradition and part of my mental preparation when competing. Come snow, wind or hail, I ride cross-country with my sleeves rolled up.

I abandoned another habit after Alexander's arrival. I had always put on my riding gloves once I was in the saddle. But one day he tried to make a run for it as I was pulling them on. They went flying and I almost went with them! Since then, I have put them on before mounting.

Now we were ready. Our class was well under way and I swung into the saddle. Alexander, who had been so excited when we arrived, was now completely laid back. I felt he was trying to look after me. It was odd that I had spent three years trying to relax him. Now it was the other way round.

There was plenty going on in the warm-up field, with ponies dashing round and leaping the practice fences. But Alexander ignored them.

We popped over a couple of jumps and he then settled to

snooze in the sun until it was our turn to go.

"Good luck,"said the lady at the start, and we trotted to the first obstacle, a tiny wooden crossbar. Alexander hopped over it and cantered away, looking for something bigger to jump. I brought him back to trot - we would need to keep at that pace to get near the optimum time. Alexander ambled along until we came to a fence and then he cantered in enthusiastically. But he obediently came back to trot after jumping. When we hurdled the final horseshoes fence, we had jumped round clear, seven seconds inside the optimum time.

"Good lad, well done,"I said, patting his neck. He tossed his head, as pleased with our efforts as I was.

I thought we had done enough to get Jenny her rosette. I was right. We were fifth. A very encouraging start.

Now for the 65cms class. This was more of a challenge. It was a longer, quite technical, course with more obstacles and lots to look at. There were two obvious potential problems - the 'skinny'fences.

Alexander had struggled with 'skinnys' from the start. The very narrow fences were the complete opposite of the hugely wide steeplechase fences he had been used to, and he was most uncomfortable with them. Today, the eighth fence was a particularly narrow tyre obstacle, and the eleventh was a skinny log. I knew he wouldn't be happy about either of them.

This time, there were more than seventy riders in the class. We would have to jump clear to have any chance of a place. As we waited our turn, I got more and more nervous. Jumping the bigger fences was a test of my mental recovery. I concentrated on psyching myself up, willing the nerves to go away. As we were called to the start, the lady in charge of the collecting ring came up and patted Alexander.

"You look after your Dad,"she said.

I was oblivious to everything except my horse. He was cool

as a cucumber, and again I felt calmed by him.

"Go when you're ready," smiled the starter.

We did one last circle and then we were off, eating up the short run to the first fence, a kind rustic crossbar. At once we were into a lovely rhythm, going at a good pace but not too fast. As I set him up for the second fence, Alexander was all ears, listening to my instructions and locking on to the obstacle. It was as if there had never been an accident. Or perhaps we were both trying to make up for it.

"The blue pipes next," I said, as we approached the fourth.

Alexander twitched his ears and focused on the blue pipes. Over we went.

We sailed over the next three fences, including a biggish log, and turned to the eighth - the skinny tyres. Alexander was bowling along enthusiastically, thoroughly enjoying himself - and then he saw the skinny. I felt his whole body tighten as a wave of anxiety swept through him.

"It's all right, lad. There's no need to worry," I said.

But now Alexander wasn't listening. He was backing off from the tyres.

I slowed to a trot, knowing my steering would have to be inch perfect and trying to give him every chance to see what he had to jump. As skinnys go, this was a particularly narrow one and the flags on either side made me feel hemmed in, never mind my horse.

"Go on, lad," I said reassuringly, trying to hold him together on a short rein and squeeze him forward with my leg. For a split second, I thought he was going to jump it. But at the last moment he ducked determinedly out to the left. I circled him and we trotted in again.

"Come on, we can do this, Alexander," I encouraged.

But the same thing happened.

I brought him round once more and gave him one smack

with my whip to try to focus him. I hardly ever use the whip on him because it upsets him so much. This time he completely ignored it. All that mattered to him was this tiny fence. I was asking him to go into a gap he clearly felt he couldn't fit through. The third attempt ended with him stopping right in front of the tyres, gawping down at them in horror. Then he began reversing away from them. He was plainly terrified and I decided enough was enough. I didn't want to spoil his day for the sake of one fence. I walked him past it and we cantered off to the next obstacle. Alexander just carried on as if nothing had happened. I really admired him for that. The skinny had frightened him, but once it was behind him, he forgot all about it.

Three fences later, we were faced with the skinny log. It wasn't quite as narrow as the tyres, and though he thought about ducking out, I rode him positively and he jumped it for me.

We went round the rest of the course in great style. Despite the trouble with the skinny, I was thrilled with the day. Alexander had given me a wonderful ride round the bigger class, confident but controlled, and that had given me the courage to ride positively. We'd had a problem at one fence. It was a genuine fear on Alexander's part and we would have to go away and practise skinnys at home.

Most importantly, Alexander's behaviour at the event had been impeccable. Jenny had been dreading taking him anywhere ever again after my terrible accident. She lay awake at night imagining him going berserk in the collecting ring at Camp Hill, with all the other horses and ponies around him. There had been a great question mark hanging in the air about whether he would set off galloping wildly out of control like that again, but I had the belief that he wouldn't, and I was right.

We rewarded Alexander by letting him munch away at the

grass next to the trailer. This time, I held his lead rope. I put my arm around his neck in a spontaneous show of affection. Then I crouched down next to him.

"You've been great today. I'm really proud of you," I said.

Alexander stopped eating and lifted his head, putting his nose to mine, as if to say: "I'm proud of you, too, Dad."

We continued to perform consistently throughout that summer and at the end of it I was amazed and proud to lift Camp Hill's 50cms series trophy. It was our first victory and could not be measured in the height of the jumps. We also came second in the final 65cms class of the season, after building our own 'skinny' at home to conquer Alexander's fear of narrow fences.

It had taken three years of hard work and we'd had lots of ups and downs, but Alexander and I now had a partnership built on the firm foundations of trust, respect and love.

Competing at Camp Hill
(Chris Lax Event Photography)

Chapter Eleven

A Bigger Stage

We finished that year on another high note when we competed for the first time at Coniston Hunter Trials. Held every autumn, it is an important and popular local event. Everyone wants to do well there. The pressure on you as a rider can be huge. It is a place where dreams can come true, or be shattered in the blink of an eye of a very public gaze. Galloping round the edge of the lake and tackling the sturdy cross-country fences is a rollercoaster ride of fear and elation. Coniston is not a place to fail, but a magical place to have success.

Against all the odds, I had twice jumped Daniel round clear in the Pairs class at Coniston. He would never have gone round on his own but with a confident lead, he had proved surprisingly up for it.

In 2008, we teamed up with Keith Rosier and his horse Salmon Loch, or Sam. I was not convinced all would go well but I didn't share Jenny's utter pessimism. She feared Daniel and I would be a disastrous combination at Coniston. I had hope, which was based on the horse's character. David Elms called Daniel 'lazy and arrogant.'It was a fair description, but within that arrogance lay my hope. I believed there was a good chance he would soak up the atmosphere and importance of the event and decide it was the big stage he deserved, and therefore perform. I hoped he would take an 'of course I can do that' attitude to the big fences. He would either love it or loathe it. There would be no in between.

I hated most of the day. Because the Pairs was the last class, it was late in the afternoon before we got our turn. The long wait was terrible. Coniston, on Daniel, was by far the biggest challenge I had faced. The fences were sizeable, solid and unforgiving. I felt physically sick and could not eat.

Loading Daniel was a nightmare. He stubbornly refused to go into the trailer. I thought my day had ended before it had begun. It took seven of us to finally shove him in. In the process, he stood on the end of my riding boot, leaving a permanent imprint. At the time it was not encouraging for the task that lay ahead, but over the years, I came to realise that when Daniel walked amicably into the trailer he usually switched off at the event. When he kicked up a fuss at loading, he tended to be up for it when we got there.

And so it proved.

When Jenny towed the trailer on to the showground and we opened the side panel, Daniel's head appeared and his neck craned to watch a competitor jumping the third fence. His ears twitched at the sound of the commentary. He was definitely interested.

I had spent most of the day shaking with nerves. But when I got on Daniel, I suddenly felt calm. The waiting was over. More than that, I could feel I had a horse beneath me, a horse that was keen and raring to go, a horse who felt that this was a place deserving of him. The arrogant bugger loved it! He was keen as mustard as we trotted round the collecting ring and hopped over the practice fence. We walked down to the start and circled round, waiting for the signal to go. Daniel could barely contain himself. At last, Keith and I were called in and the starter counted us down.

"Three-Two-One - Good luck!"

I eased the reins and Daniel shot forward enthusiastically, alongside Sam. We had eighteen obstacles to negotiate, including a spruce hurdle with a ditch in front of it, a stone wall and The Pen, where competitors jump in over one rail fence and out over another.

A successful Pairs combination will jump the fences side by side where possible. We sailed over the first fence together. It was the only one we would jump as a team. Halfway towards the second fence, a daunting ski jump, Daniel began to back off and we fell behind.

"Keep your leg on and keep him moving forward," Keith shouted back.

The nearer we got to the fence, the less Daniel liked it. It was a dramatic early test of my riding skills. I began booting Daniel furiously, then gave him one hard crack behind my leg with the whip, and twice shouted: "Get on!" It was not the place to have a stop, right in front of the commentary box, the massed crowds and the refreshment tent. With two strides to the fence, I sat back and shoved. It was now or never. And suddenly Daniel was leaping. A photo, taken from the other side of the fence, shows us coming in to land. I am still shoving. Daniel is desperately stretching out his front legs to greet the ground, his top notch of hair standing on end and a look of terror in his eyes.

It was the turning point. Daniel clearly felt that if he could jump that, he could jump anything. He happily went round, following in Sam's wake and leaping anything in front of him. After negotiating The Pen in fine style, I gave him two big pats on the neck as we headed towards the lake, making a reality of something I had dreamed of doing.

With three fences to go we cantered past the front of Coniston Hall and Daniel began to lag further behind Sam.

"Give the lazy bugger a crack!" Keith called out.

I did and Daniel responded with one last effort, picking up pace as he realised we were nearly at the finish.

We flew over the final log, as it turned out a fence from the big Open class. An official photo of the last jump shows Daniel with his front legs tucked up under his chest, his hair flying, his white socks brown from the mud and white sweat on his neck and shoulder, a very rare sight!

"This is the best day of my life," I said as Keith and I received our sixth place rosettes. It will always remain one of my finest riding achievements.

Jenny confessed to me years later that she hid in a Portaloo before the start of my round because she could not bear to witness what she was certain would be disaster and humiliation!

Taking Alexander to Coniston in 2013 was a different challenge. We would be jumping bigger fences and he was a real athlete, with power and speed and a great leap.

He showed me how well he was feeling when I went to fetch him in from his field one evening. He was grazing on the top of the hill and when I reached the gate, I called his name. His head jerked up at the sound of my voice. He looked across at me, neighed loudly and began trotting down the hill. Suddenly, he threw his head in the air, bellowed out another neigh and began galloping down the incline, his rug flapping and mud spattering everywhere.

"Steady on lad, watch your legs!" I hollered, but he charged on towards me, coming to a splashing stop in the gateway.

"Yer daft bugger,"I said, affectionately rubbing his nose as he searched me for treats.

I was feeling remarkably calm about Coniston. I suppose I was so busy at work that I hadn't had much time to think about it. Jenny and I were covering a particularly disturbing trial in which a woman was charged with the manslaughter of her four-year-old son. He had been so malnourished he starved to death and his body was left in a cot for nearly two years. The harrowing story attracted much national interest and we had to be on our toes to keep ahead of the pack of TV, radio and newspaper reporters. Jenny was queuing daily at 8.30am outside Court 3 at Bradford Crown Court to make sure she got a seat, while I was tasked with finding an 'exclusive'angle on the case. By Friday lunchtime, the mother had been found guilty and jailed for fifteen years. For the first time, I was able to think about Coniston. It was only two days away.

A couple of weeks earlier, I had received a letter from Airedale General Hospital. The CT scan I had after Alexander hurled me into the gatepost had revealed some tiny lesions on my spleen that were nothing to do with the accident. The medics said these were common, but as a precaution they wanted me to go back in six months for another scan. Here was the invitation. In one sense, I was glad to return to the hospital. I had never been back to have my injuries checked. I was told the broken bones would heal themselves and that had seemed to be the case. But in recent weeks, I'd had a few aches and twinges. They were mostly when I was in bed and I never noticed anything when I was riding. The ribs weren't painful, just a bit uncomfortable now and then.

"Maybe it's just something I'll have to live with for the rest of my life, especially in winter,"I said.

Some people suggested it could be bruising in the bones, which could take up to a year to properly come out. I wasn't concerned but I hoped another scan would confirm that all was well.

The hospital visit lasted more than two hours. I'd not been allowed to eat all day and I had to drink a jug of orange-flavoured liquid to help with the process, then sit around in a waiting room while it took effect. Eventually, the radiologist led me to the scanner room where I was injected with a dye to show up my insides.

"You will probably get a warm feeling. Don't worry. That's normal,"she said.

It was an extraordinary sensation. My throat began to glow and then the heat swept down my body to my bottom, lighting me up. It was a most peculiar feeling, though not uncomfortable.

After the long wait, the actual scan took just ten minutes. I would get an appointment to discuss the results with a consultant. For now, that was it.

The visit brought back vivid memories of the reason I had been in hospital in the first place. Now, with only forty-eight hours to wait, the challenge and the risk of Coniston was sinking in.

"I wish you were doing something else,"Jenny said.

But my mind was made up. The only question remaining was the size of fence I would choose to jump. There were three alternatives for each obstacle - small, medium and large. Small was out of the equation. I had to decide between the bigger options.

I had asked for an early start time but I was taken aback when I learned that Alexander and I were the trailblazers at 9.30am. At first it seemed a daunting prospect. All eyes would be on us as we set off. But then I began to think of the advantages. There was torrential rain during the week and the going at Coniston can get heavy. Leading off meant that the ground would not be cut up at all. And the place wouldn't be as busy as it would get later, so it would be less unsettling for Alexander. With luck, we would have a good ride round, be safe and enjoy the rest of the day.

With a day to go, my stomach was turning somersaults. I rode Alexander down the lane and I was at once at ease with the world. We had reached the stage in our relationship where we relaxed into each other. I felt safe and carefree.

"He'll soon go up a couple of gears when you need him to,"Jenny would say. And he always did. I had a sneaking feeling that he was holding plenty in reserve. As we turned for home, Alexander suddenly came alive.

"Nice and steady,"I said quietly, as a tiptoeing prance came into his gait. He bounced more as we went downhill towards the cross-country field, and as we drew level with it, he began to jog. His head twisted in hope towards the field.

"Not today, Alexander. You'll have plenty of chance to gallop about tomorrow."

We continued to bounce along the lane and I allowed him to trot purposefully home.

Jenny was waiting for us as we clattered briskly back into the yard. I grinned at her. "We've got him bang on for Coniston. He's as fit as a fiddle and raring to go."

Then it was time to walk the course. The medium sized fences were marked with blue discs, while the larger obstacles had red markers. There were only two options at the first fence, a simple two-foot log or the bigger and wider traditional rails. Take the little log and we would be setting out our stall for a safe and steady round. Jump the alternative and we would be stating our intention to push ourselves.

Keith, who walked with me, was in no doubt.

"The bigger one's an inviting fence. Alexander will jump it with his eyes shut. He could trip over the smaller one if he's careless."

It was a fair point. Alexander needed to jump bigger. On the other hand, I had to be in my comfort zone. I did not fancy some of the large fences at all but others looked within my capabilities. Medium seemed to be the best option.

"I think there are some big ones you can go for, but it's no good setting Alexander up for them if you're not committed. If in doubt - bail out!" advised Keith.

I lay awake half the night, mentally jumping round the course. Eventually, I drifted off, but I woke early, feeling physically sick, the nerves overpowering me. My head felt thick through lack of sleep. But my mind was clear. I had decided on the course I would take, subject to how we were going. It would be mostly blues, with three or four red alternatives. I was keeping my options open at a couple of the fences.

Alexander looked bright and sharp when I got to the yard. I had felt the previous day that he knew there was a competition coming up, probably picking up on my nervous energy. Now there was an edginess about him that confirmed it.

I still felt sick, but I tried to mask my terror from Alexander, mostly keeping my distance while Jenny got him ready. The last thing I wanted was for me to make him nervous. I was now delighted that we would be the first out on the course. I remembered, with no fondness at all, the sickly feeling as I waited all day to take Daniel round all those years ago.

In less than two hours, it would all be over - for better or worse.

As always, Alexander marched into the trailer and Jenny tied him up for the ten minute journey. My head was whizzing as I drove us there. The day had dawned bright and beautiful. By eight o'clock, shafts of strong, white sunlight pierced the russet trees, turning their topmost leaves into a dazzling molten copper.

As we approached the entrance to the Coniston Hotel we passed a large billboard, proclaiming 'Coniston Hunter Trials, Sunday, October 6,'and the reality kicked in.

The stewards waved us into a field at the side of the hotel and I parked up. It was 8.40am.

"I'm going to walk the course again,"I announced.

"But you need to be getting on your horse," said Jenny.

"I'm just walking the first bit. I won't be long."

I marched off in the direction of the first fence, the wet grass from the overnight dew soaking into my yard boots. As I headed towards it, I was concerned to see the bright ball of early morning sun shining directly at me. We would be looking into it for the first five fences. I prayed that it would keep climbing above eye level.

Moments later, my phone rang.

"Where are you?"asked Jenny.

"Just collecting my number. I'll be there in a minute."

As the first to go, I was given number one. I knew it wouldn't be my finishing position but I would be able to say that, barring elimination, I had led the competition.

It was time to get on my horse. I was tingling with nerves but as soon as I was in the saddle I felt better. Stewards instructed us to go past the front of the hotel and through a wood to the collecting ring. Other riders were already making their way there and we followed. As we walked along, the stress left me in waves. Just sitting on Alexander was taking it away. He had a calming effect on me and I started to focus on what we had to do.

"I am going to enjoy every moment of this,"I thought.

I drank it all in as Alexander, alert and keen, strode through the wood. As we emerged into the grounds, and the big, traditional wooden fences came into sight, he began to tug.

"I told you we'd be having fun today,"I said, as he pranced into the warm-up area.

The park looked magnificent under a dazzling blue sky. The autumn foliage glowed in the strengthening sun and fingers of mist rose from the still lake. The event was already buzzing. Wagons and trailers rolled in to park up in long lines and spectators were taking up vantage points round the course.

Smartly dressed riders were gathering in the warm-up area on their glossy and purposeful looking horses. In just a few minutes, I would be galloping round the course on my flame-coloured thoroughbred, passing by the lake and in front of Coniston Hall to the finish.

As we walked round with the other riders, the public address system suddenly burst into life and the commentator's voice boomed out across the course. Alexander stopped abruptly and stood stock still, his eyes wide. I knew what the sound reminded him of. I stretched forward and stroked his neck.

"It's all right, we're not going racing."

As if he understood, Alexander relaxed again and we continued to walk around the collecting ring.

Keith appeared. "Right. Get him going now, Steve,"he instructed.

I eased out of the saddle as Alexander moved into a positive canter. There were four or five other riders warming up in the ring. We were cantering round the edge when Alexander jinked violently to the right and tried to make a dash for it. I managed to hold him and move him forward again in a steady canter.

"It's all right. He just got a bit claustrophobic for a moment,"said Keith.

It was another reminder of why Alexander had not taken to racing. The other horses around him had unnerved him. But now he was settled again. We popped over the practice log and then I brought him in to the other practice fence, some bigger tyres. Alexander rushed in and hurdled them. Not how we should be doing it.

"If he tries that with the solid rails on the course we could come a right cropper,"I thought.

Keith, who was watching intently from the centre of the ring, called me over.

"What I want you to do is come in again and sit up, and get him to slow down and bounce."

I knew that's what I should have done the first time, but I was tense and you don't ride as well when the nerves get to you.

Keith had spotted it. "Just relax and get some bend in your elbows."

We came in again. This time I sat up and Alexander jumped it better.

"Do it once more,"said Keith.

Round we came and jumped it properly again.

"All right,"shouted Keith. "You're ready to go."

I wasn't sure if I would ever be ready. The nerves were jangling again.

Then we were called to the start and as we walked steadily down I thought about my options at the first fence. I knew which one it was to be. The bigger one. Unless I decided it was to be the smaller one, of course.

The commentator's voice was crackling across the course, but I didn't hear what he said. People were watching us, but I didn't see them. The first fence was all that mattered.

"This is it, Alexander,"I said, patting his neck.

Like me, he was staring ahead, focusing on the job in hand.

I became aware of the man at the start talking to me.

"You can go. Have a good round."

And then we were off. Alexander was cantering along, not galloping wildly. We were straight into a controlled rhythm. The fence was coming up, the two options next to each other. I pointed him at the bigger one and gave his sides a squeeze with my lower leg. And then we were up and over. We had jumped our first Coniston fence.

Jenny could not see much of the course from where she was standing, near to the start and finish, but she was reassured by the commentator's measured tones: "Adelphi Warrior is over the first, over the second... over the third and the fourth."

We dropped down neatly into the sunken road and jumped out over the wall. It was a tight turn and there wasn't much room for Alexander, but he was clever. Then we were over the shark's teeth and heading down the hill towards the lake. We cantered along the shoreline, as I had watched so many riders do in previous years, and Jenny was relieved to see the orange flash of Alexander across the water.

We began to climb towards the skinny double and I realised our course would take us beneath the thin overhanging branches of a line of trees.

"Hold tight, Alexander. We're going through,"I called.

I shut my eyes and ducked down on to his neck, the twigs brushing across the top of my hat. Alexander just kept cantering.

"You're a real professional, lad,"I said.

Now we were at the top end of the lake. The ski jump over the big, slimy ditch marked the turn for home. Neither of us noticed the scary ditch as he cleared it. Then we hit boggy ground. Alexander likes it to be firm but he just pulled his hooves out of the clinging surface and kept going.

We passed the imposing hall and I knew we were in the closing stages. There was just the tricky water complex to negotiate before the final fence. A wide rail took us on to a steep bank which we dropped off into the water and then we jumped out over another rail. It was a testing event combination, but Alexander went through it as if he had been doing it for years.

It takes five or six minutes to jump round the Coniston course but it seems to be over in the blink of an eye. You have to think quickly as you go round and adapt to circumstances, and to how well you are going. The concentration is intense. Before you know it, you have reached the end, and only then can you relax.

As we turned for the final fence the left rein slipped from my grasp, tiredness grabbing a tighter hold than that of my hand. But Alexander didn't panic, and he waited while I gathered up the reins.

We straightened up and approached the last. We had jumped twenty one fences safely. Just one more and we would have the clear round I had dreamed about. It was an Open fence, a hanging log, but the smallest red on the course, and when we had walked it, Keith and I had instantly agreed it was the one to jump.

As we came into it, I remembered Keith's words.

"The fence has no log in front of it to give it a ground line. The horse could get under it, especially if he is tired at the end of the course, and trip over it. Make sure you have him bouncing at it, so that he gets the height."

I followed his advice and Alexander jumped it nicely. We surged through the finish. We were clear! And I had enjoyed every moment.

The course is on a big loop and, as we galloped along, the first fence came back into view ahead of us. It seemed only seconds ago that we were setting out towards it. Alexander clocked it and, instead of pulling up, he increased his tempo, clearly fancying another spin round the course. We swept past a lady holding out a red and gold completion rosette in her outstretched hand. As we thundered by, Jenny dashed forward, determined we should not miss out on our prize.

"I'll take that," she said.

I hauled Alexander to a halt and, after patting and praising him, began to walk him away from the course. He was reluctant to go. I had predicted Coniston would be perfect for him, and he had loved it. The fences had been nothing to him.

I had decided to play safe and jump mainly the middle-sized blue fences. They were big enough, at around 2ft 9ins high, and wide and solid. I knew we would be nowhere near the six places on offer so it was all about getting round clear and safe. We had done that.

I dismounted to spare Alexander but he seemed to have more than enough energy for another circuit. His eyes rolled and his chestnut coat was black with sweat. I wearily trotted beside him as he marched me back to the trailer park, snatching at the reins and tossing his head in excitement.

The last eight months had been an incredible journey that had taken me from the pain of crushed ribs and shattered confidence to the joy of jumping round tough cross-country courses with a horse who was my soulmate. Alexander had changed in three years from an uncertain, slightly bonkers young thoroughbred, fresh from the racecourse, to a trusted and gentle companion and a talented competing partner. My big orange friend; how proud I was of him, and how happy he made me.

Two years later, we flew round Coniston again, this time jumping mostly the big fences. The man who started us that day was leading Hunt member John Chadwick.

In 2017, John would be a race rival.

Chapter Twelve

Fence Judging

The rolling countryside where our race would be run is also the location for Skipton Horse Trials, an important British Eventing one-day event. Top local riders, as well as one or two well-known professionals, compete there.

The horse trials need dozens of unpaid volunteers to help them run smoothly and one year Sophie and I were asked to be cross-country fence judges. Our role was to decide whether each horse and rider cleared the obstacle correctly, time them and log every detail on a form. We had to maintain contact via walkie talkie with a control centre, keep the course clear of spectators when galloping horses approached, and make sure the fence and ground were safe for the competitors. Our radio reports to the control room were instantly broadcast by the commentators, keeping spectators informed of the progress of the riders on the course.

Fence judges may also be called upon to stop a competitor or deal with a fallen horse or rider. It is a highly responsible and vital role.

Some of this I knew when I volunteered. Much of it I didn't, but Sophie and I were under no illusions after an hour-long breakfast-time briefing.

Controller Adam Bennett would be the man on the other end of the walkie talkie if we had a crisis to deal with. I hoped we wouldn't need to have a conversation. When the briefing ended I sat in my white plastic chair, clutching our pack of vital accessories - the red flag one of us would have to bravely wave in front of a galloping horse if we had to stop it, the whistle we would have to blow to prevent an unaware family being trampled to death, and the walkie talkie we might have to use to summon the paramedics or the horse ambulance - and wondered what we had let ourselves in for. That was without thinking about the possibility of a top rider querying one of our judgements and us having to appear before the committee to explain our decision. I glanced across the table at Sophie. Our eyes met and I wondered if mine held the same look of terror.

We stood up and queued for our packed lunch. I shovelled ham salad and cheese and tomato sandwiches, fruit, cake and biscuits into my brown paper bag and mused whether I would have the time or the inclination to eat them.

As we left the marquee, I whispered to Sophie: "It's a hell of a responsibility." She nodded nervously.

I looked at my watch. It was 9.20am.

"My God!"I exclaimed. "The first rider sets off in half an hour and we don't even know where our fence is!"

We got directions and set off, snaking our way from field to field until at last we reached our location. It was the final fence in the first class, the BE100. It shouldn't present any problems. If the competitors had gone round the rest of the course, they ought to jump the last. The fence was parallel with the first jump, and just a few yards away.

It was time to get ready for the first competitor. There were only minutes to go.

Sophie and I had agreed our roles. She would blow the whistle to warn of the approaching riders, and log each competitor's time and whether or not they had jumped clear. I would use the stopwatch, and inform the controller on the walkie talkie of how each rider had fared. The red flag would be my responsibility, if we had to use it.

My first job was to pick out a point, around fifty yards in front of the fence, at which to press the button on the stopwatch to record every rider's time. A gateway seemed perfect.

The controller had already been in contact to check that everyone's radio was working. Suddenly, his voice crackled out again.

"Fence judges, the first competitor is about to start the course."

This was it. Out of the corner of my eye, I saw a horse and rider jumping the first fence, just to our left. The radio burst into life.

"Horse Number One, clear at the first fence."

Nicky Green and Opening Bid II were on their way. In about twelve minutes they would be approaching our fence.

The radio crackled into life in my hand. I heard a woman's calm and controlled voice.

"Number One clear at Fence 17 A and B."

I looked down the course. A horse and rider appeared. Nicky Green and Opening Bid II were here. The bay gelding sprang over the eighteenth obstacle and galloped on towards the nineteenth fence. Our fence. Now I could hear the horse's hooves as they thundered on the turf. I fiddled nervously with the stopwatch, my finger poised above the stop button.

The warning shrill of a whistle shrieked out next to me. Sophie was right on cue. Now it was my turn. I eyed the rider, feeling slightly uncomfortable as I peered at her chest to check her number. I needn't have worried. The young lady was completely unaware of me. Her focus was on our fence, her last one.

The horse passed the gatepost, and my finger came down

on the stop button. I heard a beep, telling me I had recorded the time correctly. I focused again on the rider, who was now setting up to jump our fence. It was made of solid, sloping planks of wood, painted pale blue and white, with a row of boxed flowers in front of it. It looked wide but inviting. I thought it wouldn't cause many problems for riders of this calibre.

I imagined galloping towards it on Alexander. How would we deal with it? I felt sure Alexander would fly it, probably standing off and putting in a big leap.

Nicky Green and Opening Bid II jumped the fence well. We had no judgement call to make.

"Number One clear at Fence 19,"I said into the walkie talkie.

There was no response from the commentator. I suddenly realised I hadn't held down the grey button. It meant nobody could hear me. I tried again.

"Number One clear at Fence 19,"I repeated.

"Number 100 clear at Fence 12,"the radio replied.

"Am I doing this right?"I thought, beginning to panic.

Then the voice of David Horton in the commentary box came booming across the course.

"And Nicky Green and Opening Bid have cleared the final fence and completed their round."

Thank God.

"What was the time, Dad?"asked Sophie, clipboard in hand.

"Oh yes. Erm. Ten-One-Eleven,"I said, reading the hour, minute and second I had recorded.

I breathed a sigh of relief. One down. How many to go? Don't bother counting, there's too many.

The next rider was soon upon us, and jumping our fence. We went through our routine. Whistle, stopwatch, walkie talkie, clipboard. Reassuringly, David Horton instantly announced that the rider had finished.

The horses were coming through at regular three or four minute intervals. We were getting into a rhythm. Whistle, stopwatch, walkie talkie, clipboard. David. Whistle, stopwatch, walkie talkie, clipboard. David.

All was going well.

Then I noticed Sophie staring across to the collecting ring where riders were warming up their horses before the start.

"I think that's Ruth Edge,"she announced.

Skipton attracts a few international event riders, bringing their young horses learning their trade. Ruth Edge, a regular at four-star events like Badminton and Burghley, was one of them.

Sophie looked over more intently. "Yes, it is,"she confirmed.

I grabbed the event programme and skimmed through the list of riders. And there she was. Ruth Edge. Not just once, but four times.

"Oh my God. The last thing we want is her taking out a flag and us having to judge whether we should penalise her,"I groaned.

But, of course, when she reached our fence she sailed effortlessly over it. We hardly had time to admire a star in action before the next competitor was heading our way. They were coming thick and fast, but we had relaxed and were starting to enjoy ourselves. I noticed that, while some of the fence judges simply stuck to the basic information that was needed, others were playing to the commentary.

"Number Three flies Fence Six,""Number 14 is a little reluctant but clear at Fence Ten,"and "Number 116 is clear at Fence Eight, with lots of encouragement from the rider!"were immediately relayed to the spectators by the commentators.

Soon I was joining in. I realised that the more information I gave, the more colourful the commentary would be. But I also had in mind that if I was anxiously waiting for news of a loved one as they made their way round the course, I would want to know they were safe. I resolved that I would not deliver bad news unless it was absolutely necessary. There was no need, as everyone jumped our fence safely. I was even able to report that one lady rider whooped with joy on completing the course.

Lunchtime was passing and I had just started to nibble at my bag of goodies when the class came to an end. We found ourselves being moved further back up the course for the bigger Novice class. This time, we were judging at a large and wide double of roll tops, with the two obstacles set at an angle. The riders would have a downhill approach to the fences.

"This looks more challenging. I think we'll have more to do here,"I said.

I could see the potential for horses running out at the second part of the double and us having to make plenty of judgement calls. But the riders tackled it sensibly and skilfully and there was just one run out. The only hiccup was when I failed to press the stopwatch properly for one rider and had to guess the time. I had glanced at the watch before stopping it, so I had a good idea of what it was. And, anyway, we were only a very small cog in the wheel of accuracy.

I was becoming more ambitious with my descriptions for the commentary. One rider 'rattled'both parts of the double, while another 'rode brilliantly'to get over the second part. I was chuffed to hear both my comments quickly relayed to the crowd.

I was getting the impression that some fence judges were trying to outdo the others, particularly the ones at the last fence, who happened to be from our yard. I noticed that if a rider jumped our fence 'nicely,'they cleared the last 'very nicely.'And where they 'flew' our fence, they 'absolutely flew' the final jump. My suspicions were confirmed in the marquee afterwards, as we all enjoyed a free tea and wine to celebrate the success of the day. The young lady who was judging at the last admitted: "Every time we heard you getting descriptive, we had to go one better!"

Chapter Thirteen

On The Gallops

After two weeks of race training we were trotting or cantering up the track half a dozen times each session. Most of the time I was managing to stand up in the stirrups to strengthen the muscles in my lower legs. Crouching over my tall thoroughbred as he powered along, I was an unwelcome sight to ladies at the yard hacking gently by.

"Is Steve out riding on the track?" they would ask Jenny, not wanting to be suddenly confronted by a snorting and puffing Alexander on a sharp uphill bend.

Riders were also keeping a watchful eye out for us in Posh School, where I had begun our fast circuit training. I had calculated that ten laps round the school on both reins worked out at about 1.6 miles - well over the race distance. I stood up in the stirrups, leaning forward over Alexander's neck as we cantered round and round the arena. I was riding two holes shorter to get used to being in the jockey position. It actually felt quite comfortable, but it was hard work and I had to take a break halfway through our first schooling session.

"I'll have to get fitter," I told Jenny. "I won't be able to stop for a rest halfway through the race!"

The fields, which in places had been a quagmire after a long, wet winter, had begun to dry out, allowing us to start doing faster work on grass. I chose a gently sloping meadow.

Alexander was keen to attack it. After three brisk uphill runs he was puffing. When we got back to the yard he was sweated up and had white snot in his nostrils, showing he was getting a good blow and clearing out his system.

"Ian would be pleased with that," I thought.

Alexander was still enthusiastically trotting back to the yard after finishing our work, but during our sessions he was controlled and professional. He seemed relaxed about returning to race training. Friends commented on how happy he was in his stable, where he could be a bit of a grump. Working seemed to be making him more content and even playful, a notion met with cynicism by Jenny after he bit her hard on the leg when she was undoing his outdoor rug. The savage attack came totally without warning as she put her hands on the front buckle. Alexander had always snapped his teeth when being girthed and when his rugs were adjusted but he had never actually bitten anyone before. The shock and searing pain made Jenny feel sick and faint and she was left with a massive, black swollen bruise on her thigh. It was weeks before she felt able to skip Alexander out without putting a head collar on him and she is still cautious about turning her back on him in the stable.

One afternoon, after a vigorous canter session, Alexander and I stood together in the sun. I stroked his neck while he amused himself by playing with the sweat scraper and bucket. If it was possible, the race training was bringing us even closer together.

It was now only seven weeks to the race and time to step up our training. I needed to find somewhere where we could canter over a longer distance. I opted for the all-weather gallops at Crow Wood Equestrian Centre, near Burnley. The last time we had been there, five years ago, Alexander got over excited and bucked me off. Jenny feared the result could be the same this time, so we chose to go without another horse, hoping that would keep him calm.

Alexander seemed to confirm Jenny's fears when he emerged from our horse wagon. He was really on his toes and somehow seemed to remember that this was a place where he could gallop. But I felt confident, and as soon as I got on him he seemed to relax, happy in the knowledge that this time we could have fun together.

The gallops are half a mile long and meander in a circle around thin copses of trees and within sight and sound of a motorway.

There was a spring in Alexander's step as we walked to them but he was well behaved, not even bothering about a noisy five-a-side football match being played nearby.

We had the gallops to our ourselves, and it was reassuring that there were no other horses to fuel his competitive spirit. I walked him round the first circuit to keep him chilled, and he was content to wait for my signal but as we started our second lap we moved straight into canter. There was no silliness from Alexander and we happily lobbed along for two circuits of the track, about a mile in distance, without stopping, an encouraging indication of my level of fitness.

After a brief rest, we did a further three laps, with short breaks in between, and I kicked him into a faster canter on the last stretch, before calling it a day. Alexander was sweating and blowing a little, but his exertions did not seem to have taken too much out of him. It was clear he was already fairly fit, but that wasn't too surprising, considering how busy we kept ourselves. During the summer, we went out twice a month, competing in hunter trials, one-day events and showjumping, while we concentrated on indoor showjumping through the winter.

Alexander's behaviour was encouraging. There had been no hint of rebellion or over exuberance. In fact, he had been remarkably relaxed. Even when I asked him for the fast canter, he showed no desire to tear off in a crazy gallop. Instead, I had to encourage him to keep up to his work, which was a good test of my fitness. In total, we had cantered two and a half miles, and had done it easily enough. Afterwards I gave him a shower and shampoo and he stood happily to dry in the sun. It wasn't what I had expected. I thought I would have my hands full on the gallops. It seemed that, at thirteen, he had grown up.

Back at the yard, Jenny got out the scissors and shortened Alexander's tail. When she saw Emilly Thane, she couldn't resist quipping: "Five circuits on the gallops, and a Cheltenham-style tail! One-nil to us!"

Emilly and I were rooting for each other and sharing early anxieties over the race. But we were also developing a robust friendly rivalry, each questioning what training the other was doing. When Emilly took Joe out in her wagon, I became suspiciously inquisitive. And she grilled Jenny when one of my training sessions showed no sign of coming to an end.

"I know what he's like. He'll be taking it very seriously," Emilly observed.

We had agreed to sponsor each other for £20. Emilly looked bewildered when I handed her a £20 note.

"What do we do now? Do I give you this back?" she asked.

"No," I replied. "You put that in a plastic container and give me another £20 note!"

A couple of weeks later, I took Alexander back to Crow Wood. This time, Emilly and Joe came with us.

"He's going to have to run with other horses in the race," I said to Jenny. "We need to see how he copes in training."

Again, he surprised me by taking it all in his stride. He walked beside the other horse for half a circuit of the track before moving into a fast canter. Alexander began alongside Joe, but then dropped himself in behind and was happy to bowl along in his slipstream while we cantered three circuits, or one and a half miles. For the last furlong we increased the pace to gallop. Alexander continued to happily stalk Joe, only going past him as the horses pulled up.

I was delighted. Alexander had felt fantastic. He seemed very comfortable with the fast work and I got the impression he had a lot more in reserve, had I wanted it. On our last circuit he got the bit between his teeth and began to throw his head around, wanting to go faster. But he immediately accepted it when I refused his request. It was a great confidence booster, knowing he was willing to listen even though he was brimming with enthusiasm. Perhaps I would have the same control in the race.

I was pleased that I was hardly puffing at the end. I was getting fitter and I was beginning to believe that both of us could be physically ready by race day.

I continued to receive good advice from friends. Michael McNeela had been a work rider and conditional jockey for top trainers Gordon Richards and Nicky Henderson, riding two Grand National winners, Corbiere and Lucius, in training.

"Keep Alexander relaxed in the parade ring," he said. "You could lose the race if he burns up too much energy by getting over-excited. And look for the good ground when you walk the course.

"I would keep him handy in the race and see what he has got left for the final couple of furlongs."

Michael added: "It won't be your last race. You'll get bitten by the bug!"

I could see how that might happen.

When the Cheltenham Festival came round again, I watched it on the television with Keith and his partner, Nicola. On one of the days we were joined by local point-to-point trainer Wendy Wild. She had helped to train a young Daniel and had rounded him up on many occasions when he was running loose at Craven Country Ride after dumping his rider.

"I would feed Alexander three times a day," Wendy advised.

"You want to do plenty of standing trots for your legs, and shorten your stirrups. It will help to secure your lower legs in case something jinks and comes across you, or barges into you.

"You'll only need to get a couple of gallops into him in the last week before the race."

Wendy added: "Don't push him up the hill on the racecourse, it's steep. Let him go up at his own pace."

Her words reminded me of the hazardous quest I had embarked on. By now, a plan was forming in my head as to how I would ride the race. I was concerned about how Alexander would react to having other horses around him so I wanted to keep him clear of the rest of the runners. The best option seemed to be to jump him off away from the pack and then ease him back to save his energy, keeping him out wide.

Chapter Fourteen

The Fragile Thoroughbred

Six weeks before the race, Alexander came in injured from the field. He had suffered a cut to the inside of his hind leg, just above the hoof, while gadding about with his pals. It did not appear to be serious but it had sliced right through the skin and could become a problem if we did not look after it.

I managed to joke about it with Emilly, suggesting her horse had encouraged Alexander to misbehave in the field.

Emilly, who had washed and dried Alexander's wound before spraying it with antiseptic, retorted: "I have given him an extra-large haynet tonight so that he'll be too fat to run!"

But despite the banter, I was worried. It was my biggest fear that Alexander would get injured and not make it to the race. He had frequently been out of action over the years after hurting himself in the field. Thoroughbreds have a reputation for being fragile and easily damaged and Alexander is his own worst enemy. He loves to play with his friends but when he gets too boisterous, accidents can happen. He runs about when the other horses have settled to graze, chasing after them, rearing up in front of them and tugging mischievously at their rugs. That is when he becomes a nuisance and can get kicked.

Alexander's injuries are usually minor, and more frustrating than damaging, but just four months after I bought him, his antics almost cost him his life.

At the time, I was still trying to understand him. He was a cool customer and didn't give much away about what he was thinking and feeling, but he was restful to be with. It was a subtle process to fall in love with a horse like him. He didn't demand to be loved. But his fragility and vulnerability drew me in. I wanted to wrap my arms around his long, orange neck and give him a hug, so I did. His response was neither to object, nor to welcome the hugs, but simply to accept them.

I was walking along the platform at Leeds Railway Station after reporting on a case at the city's Crown Court, when I got the phone call from Jenny. It was hard to hear what she was saying above the hubbub of commuters and noisy station announcements. But what was all too clear was the awful upset and panic in her voice.

And then her words registered: "Alexander's been badly injured."

He had put his hind leg through a post and rail fence in the field, dragged it out and cut it badly. How badly was not clear, but his blood was everywhere and he was standing on three legs. The rest of the herd had kept their distance, except for Daniel, who had stayed protectively at his side. The vet was on her way. Until then we could only guess horribly about how it might end.

I carried on with my journey in a complete whirl. Nothing mattered but Alexander's well being. I felt sick to the stomach, as if I had been poisoned. My pride and joy was wounded, possibly fatally. Horses have strong but delicate legs and there is a limit to what can be done to repair them. Medical and technological advances and veterinary skills have pushed out the recovery boundaries. But there are still too many sad cases where nothing can be done and the only humane course is to have the horse put down. Facing that possibility, my mind was clear about how much Alexander meant to me. He was everything. I was distraught. Things were made worse by my feeling of utter helplessness. I was thirty miles away. My car was halfway up the railway line to home and it would take up to two hours to get back to the yard. There was nothing I could do but wait for news. But I knew that when the next phone call came, it might be to tell me that Alexander was dead.

When the phone rang, it brought me hope. The vet had examined Alexander, bandaged his leg and led him down from the field. He had been taken to the Equine Clinic at Rathmell, near Settle. The fact that Alexander had been able to walk into the trailer was massively good news. He had got over the first huge hurdle.

Alexander was alive. Now all I wanted was to see him but it was too late to go that day. Hospital visiting hours were long over and the patients would be settled for the night. I would have to wait until I got through the next day in the office.

When I got to the hospital, Alexander was munching on a pile of hay in a stable overlooking the equine swimming pool. His injured leg was encased in a large red bandage but he seemed to be at ease and he was moving round well.

"Now then, lad. How are you?" I asked cheerily.

He peered round at me and carried on eating his tea. Not so bad, it seemed.

With the hospital staff about to do their evening rounds, I had only a few minutes to spend with him, but I was allowed to give him a couple of small treats and I left feeling reassured that he was settled and comfortable. At the weekend I was able to go for a longer visit. Just as I reached his stable, the vet arrived to change his bandage. I walked steadily with Alexander to the examination room, around the edge of the pool. He was sedated before the bandage was changed. I stood holding his head collar, ready to support him. As the drug began to take effect, his head started to sink until his chin rested on my chest. His eyes were glazing over and occasionally his head jerked as he tried to stay awake, like a little old man nodding off in his chair in front of the fire. It was a tender few moments. Alexander was so large and yet so fragile, but I was there for him. We stood with our heads together and I couldn't have felt closer to him.

When the bandage was removed I saw the injury for the first time. The skin and flesh at the front of his near hind leg, just below the hock joint, had been ripped away, cutting him to the bone and slicing through his extensor tendon, leaving a gaping wound. It had been cleaned and bandaged, and he had been given antibiotics and painkillers.

It was obviously a very serious injury. Alexander had survived it but I was unclear about the healing process and his future prospects. While the vet seemed happy with the wound, and the X-rays of it, he remained non-committal about Alexander's long term recovery.

Alexander was discharged from the hospital after eight days and it was uplifting to see his head looking out over his stable door when I arrived at the yard. He seemed happy to show off his large, bright red bandage, peering round as if to admire it.

Vet Joe McKinder was in charge of Alexander's care. He was thorough and had a relaxed and caring approach to his patients. I knew my horse was in good hands. Joe visited Alexander regularly and at first he was pleased with his progress. But after several days there was no sign of the wound knitting together. The healing process seemed to have stalled. A week after Alexander's homecoming, Joe decided to remove the bandage in the hope that the fresh air circulating around the wound would kick-start the healing. Nothing happened.

Sixteen days after Alexander had come home, Joe called me at work. He had examined him again and he was now seriously concerned by the lack of improvement. Joe wanted to try something different. I was happy for him to do whatever was necessary. I just wanted my horse to be fit again.

Joe's plan was to flush out the wound with a sterile liquid squeezed into the injury site out of special bags. He hoped this would remove anything buried deep down that might be causing infection and preventing recovery. His idea appeared to work. For a few days there were clear signs of improvement. The wound began to stop its endless seeping of gunk, and healthy skin seemed to be developing. Then the recovery process ground to a halt. The wound stubbornly refused to close and it resumed its leaking of yellow pus. Alexander was not out of the woods. It was more than six weeks since he had injured himself and he still wasn't mending.

Joe now arranged for veterinary surgeon Peter Schofield to take a look at Alexander at Hird & Partners equine hospital, near Halifax. When we got there, Alexander bounced out of the trailer. He was lathered in sweat, his long neck strained as he took in his new surroundings, and he refused to stand still as I held him on his lead rope. I was asked to walk him up and down and it was all I could do to hang on to him as he snorted and tugged.

Alexander was taken to the examination room where his injured leg was shaved and he was given an ultrasound test. It revealed that there was a foreign body in the wound. My worst fears were realised. He needed an operation under general anaesthetic. It would take place the next day.

Any surgery on a horse, as with humans, carries a risk. There is always the possibility of a reaction to the anaesthetic. Like us, some horses react worse than others and can die. All I could do was go home and hope that I would see Alexander again.

The following day seemed to go on forever. I had been told

the operation would take several hours and not to expect any news until the late afternoon. Jenny and I tried to occupy ourselves at the livery yard but it was impossible to keep Alexander, and what was happening to him, out of our thoughts. The afternoon dragged on. We placed Jenny's phone in front of us, willing it to ring. But it remained silent. The time crawled by. We had hoped to hear something by four o'clock. Four thirty came and went. By 4.40pm, Jenny was starting to panic. The later it got the more convinced she was that Alexander was dead.

At last, the phone rang. I looked at Jenny for some clue in her face. And then she said: "Thank God,"and I knew Alexander was alive.

Veterinary surgeon Tim Booth had carried out keyhole surgery to get deep into the wound where debris had buried itself beyond the reach of our vet. He had removed a number of rotten tendon fragments and other bits of rubbish from the injury. No wonder it hadn't healed.

Tim was confident the wound would now mend quickly. Alexander could be back in action in a matter of weeks.

When the thoroughbred first came into my life, Jenny had made a gloomy prediction.

"It will get broken, be on box rest for three months and you'll have to get back on it in the middle of winter."

Her forecast was proving spot on.

Four days after his operation, we brought Alexander home. He remained confined to his stable but I soon saw signs of pink skin growing and the wound knitting together. He really was getting better. This time the recovery continued. As the days and weeks went by, the improvement gathered pace. Alexander was a good patient. For the most part, he was relaxed and dealt with his confinement better than most horses. In the week before Christmas, Joe McKinder discharged him from his care.

Alexander was fully recovered but he still bears the scars.

He suffered another nasty injury soon after moving to Farfield.

Charles phoned me one afternoon.

"Alexander's been kicked," he said. "Don't worry. I don't think it's too bad but our vet, Michael Bradley, is on his way."

Michael was with Alexander when I got to the yard.

"Whatever have you done now?" I asked my horse, in concerned exasperation.

He had suffered a hefty blow to the right elbow. There was a cut, which did not look serious, but the joint was swollen. It was not a good place to have an injury. Problems with the elbow joint can prove irreparable in the wrong circumstances. Alexander had been given an anaesthetic and he stood dopily as I stroked his face while Michael completed his examination.

The vet finally stepped away and I looked in his eyes, searching for clues about how bad it might be.

"What's the verdict?" I asked.

Michael stood thoughtfully for a few seconds. I waited. At last he spoke.

"The wound is one centimetre deep and then it goes upwards. My concern is that it has gone into the elbow joint, which would not be good. My gut feeling is that it has penetrated the layers of muscle and not quite reached the joint itself. But I can't be sure yet."

He added that it was unlikely the elbow was fractured or cracked - but he could not rule it out.

"I'll come back in the morning and see how he is," Michael said.

"I'm not going to give him any painkillers because I don't want them to mask anything when I re-examine him. I'll talk to you after that. If he is walking soundly on it, then it will just be a case of giving him antibiotics and he will recover speedily.

If not, we may have to consider X-rays."

I stood with Alexander, our heads together, and stroked his neck. I stared into space, my mind racing, praying that he would be all right. He was starting to come round. He seemed quite perky and not in any serious discomfort.

"You'll be fine, won't you lad?"

He met my anxious gaze with a look of confidence and I felt reassured. But the news from Michael was not good the following morning.

"He is walking well, but there's fluid coming from the wound and he has pain around the elbow. I want to refer him to hospital."

Michael tried to reassure me.

"It's probably not very serious, but I want to be sure. If we left him and then in a couple of days, he was dog lame and we couldn't move him, there would be nothing we could do for him. I couldn't look you in the face again if there was something we could have done to save him."

I saw the sense of that and steeled myself for Alexander to be taken again to Hird and Partners. Charles towed him there and phoned to tell me he had arrived safely. Now I waited to hear from the hospital. The call was not long in coming and the news was positive. An X-ray had revealed that Alexander had chipped the bone on the end of the elbow. He would be pumped full of antibiotics to prevent infection and stay at Hird's for three to four days. Then he would return home for two weeks of box rest before being allowed out in a small paddock for a fortnight. After that, he would be X-rayed again to see how the injury was progressing.

After work, we made the familiar trip out of Bradford to the hospital. Alexander was in a high dependency stable. He had a tube for administering drugs attached to his neck, which was partially shaved, as was the top of his injured leg. He was cosy and seemed to be in no discomfort but he looked a little sorry for himself, pressing his nose against the stable bars to watch us go.

Before leaving, we spoke to surgeon Tim Booth. He showed us the X-rays and we could clearly see the chip separated from the bone.

"There are two things we hope could happen," Tim told us.

"Either the chip dissolves and is absorbed, or it re-aligns itself to the bone. But because of the position of the injury, my best guess is that neither of those will happen and he will have to come back for surgery to remove the chip."

He added: "Either way, he will definitely make a full recovery."

I was buoyed by Tim's words. Although I did not want Alexander to undergo surgery, the fact was he would get better.

"Oh well," Jenny reflected. "It's been at least eighteen months since one of you was last in hospital!"

I visited Alexander again the next day. I went into his stable and patted his neck.

"Don't worry, lad," I told him. "We'll sort this together – we always do."

The second X-ray showed that the chip of bone had dissolved. Alexander did not need surgery and he could be ridden again.

He had plenty of energy after his lay off. We had moved to Farfield only two months earlier and I was still in awe of the magnificent views from the hilltops, stretching from Ilkley's Cow and Calf rock formation to Bolton Abbey. Alexander trotted effortlessly up the steep track and into the pasture leading to the Pepsi Max field, so-called because its dizzyingly steep undulations resemble the rollercoaster ride at Blackpool Pleasure Beach. The ground was very soft and I didn't want to churn it up, so I stuck to the stony path in the middle. Halfway up, I let Alexander canter steadily to the top. Then I turned him round and walked back down.

"Shall we go up again?" I asked.

The question needed no answer, beyond the fast canter Alexander immediately broke into. It was clearly an invitation he could not refuse and after a few strides, he went into gallop. I didn't mind, not even when he threw in a small buck. His pent-up energy needed some sort of release. But I cautiously eased him back to a canter, and we pulled up at the gate. Alexander was now excited and bounced and jogged back down the track, prancing and snorting. I sat back, shoved my feet forward and relaxed the reins, determined to enjoy the jig-jogging exuberance of a pure thoroughbred. This was what having Alexander was all about, making the most of these moments of athleticism and enthusiasm that come with such a horse. I felt an inner warmth and happiness and could sense Alexander's contentment. It was a memorable ride in beautiful countryside. And we were together. Man and horse as one kindred spirit. What could be better?

Alexander's latest injury was not nearly so serious but with the race looming up, I couldn't afford to take any chances.

We had qualified for the semi-finals of the national Trailblazers showjumping competition but I kept Alexander at home over the weekend because it wasn't worth the risk. Trailblazers could wait for another year. We might not get another chance at a race. Instead, Alexander stayed in his stable. I didn't even want him out in the field in case mud got into the wound and caused an infection. A couple of days off at this stage should not make any difference.

We resumed our training on the Monday and three days later, Michael came to the yard to check Alexander's cut.

"He doesn't need antibiotics," he said. "Spray the wound

twice a day and keep him in. But keep working him, there's no problem with that."

"While you're here, would you check his heart?" I asked.

Michael listened carefully to Alexander's heart and airwaves for several minutes.

"His heartbeat is perfectly normal," he said.

"When you listen to it, it goes lub-blub, dub; lub-blub, dub. That is exactly how it should sound!"

It was reassuring that Alexander was in good health, but I couldn't help but worry. There is always a risk when racing.

I couldn't bear it if anything went wrong.

There is a lot of nonsense talked about racing being cruel. It isn't. In fact, few horses are better treated or more loved and cared for than racehorses. But racing is dangerous – for both horse and jockey – and, tragically, there are fatalities on the racecourse.

Horses are fragile animals and the sad truth is they are much more likely to die at home, galloping about in the field. They can be killed by a kick from another horse, or simply while running around having fun. I could easily have lost Alexander when he ripped open his leg on the fence. And all too often they are victims of terrible illness. We have endured the awful pain of losing a horse who was a much-loved member of the family, a beautiful and talented young mare. A star who should have shone brightly for many years.

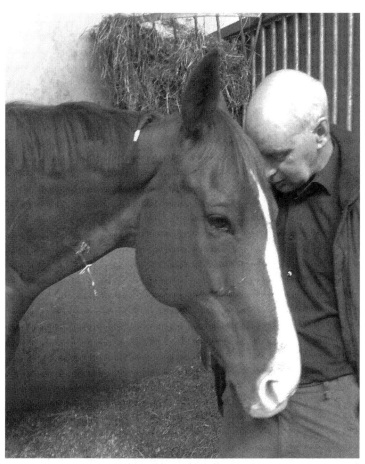

Visiting Alexander in hospital

Chapter Fifteen

Innes

A year after we bought Alexander, we went to Grange-over-Sands to learn more about his background from Ian and Karen Conroy.

After chatting and looking round the yard where he had lived, we took a stroll up the fields, high above the spectacular estuary, to see the couple's young horses. They were a contented and handsome looking bunch, quality animals that anyone would want to buy. More than one caught our eye, in particular a small, stocky, jet black mare who was very busy and keen to push her way to the front and be noticed.

"There's me!"she seemed to say.

She was an Irish part thoroughbred, not yet three years old. Her mother, who was also at the stud farm, was a retired racehorse called Goldengirlmichelle who had won three hurdle races. Her dad was the famous event stallion Jumbo, whose offspring included Badminton Horse Trials winner Hedley Britannia. Consequently, Ian and Karen had nicknamed her Nellie.

Jenny could not get Nellie out of her head. Her favourite horse, the black Irish mare, Dark Autumn, was leaving for a new life with Jenny's daughter. Here, perhaps, was a little horse who could give her fresh hope and purpose.

"She's my perfect horse, Steve,"she said.

And so she bought her. A week before Jenny's 54th birthday, Nellie arrived in a trailer with Ian and Karen. A violent storm flared, with thunder and lightning, just as they were expected. But it blew over and the sun came out to welcome them. A little black bundle of energy came bounding out of the trailer and tugged Ian off towards the canal bridge. We put Nellie with Dark Autumn in a small paddock and watched anxiously as she explored her little field. She did not seem at all worried by her new surroundings and had the same vitality and purpose we had noticed the first time we saw her.

Nellie joined the herd of mares at the stables and soon teamed up with an ex-racehorse called Cinders. They were often to be found lying down together.

Like me with Alexander, Jenny wanted to give Nellie a name of her own. Because she was small, black and Irish, she called her Innes – half of Guinness.

Although classily bred, Innes was a bouncing, muddy bundle of fluff. Jenny adored her and spent ages simply admiring her. Jet black from head to foot, the little mare had athletic racehorse legs, a stocky neck and an Irish barrel belly. Barely 15.1 hands high, she exuded a bustling joy of living. Innes settled in straight away, embracing the activity of a busy livery yard. She gawped at other horses as they were ridden past her stable or were cantered in the school. It seemed as if she could not wait to grow up and join in. She loved people and was a delight to be with.

Jenny spoilt the little mare with treats and new clothes and blingy accessories. Her head collar was trimmed with white fur and her smart black grooming brushes had shimmering gold bristles. Friends chided Jenny for being too soft with her, and the youngster's smug and pampered expression as she looked over her stable door showed she had no doubt who was in charge.

We backed Innes that autumn, with the help of friends, and she came on in leaps and bounds – literally. When we let her loose in the lunging pen one day, she went crackers, bucking herself inside out. Round and round she whizzed, her head between her knees and her heels flying above our heads.

"Oh my God," said Jenny. "Someone's got to get on that. And it isn't going to be me!"

Innes always had plenty of spirit. Karen told us how the mare jumped out of the field when she was a few months old, followed by her anxious mother and the other mares and foals.

"That's making a nice shape," remarked a friend, as the black foal sailed over the three-foot-high electric tape.

"Never mind the shape, it's off!" replied Karen.

Naughty little Innes led the other horses along the esplanade to the centre of Grange-over-Sands, where they made a circuit of the Clock Tower and headed back home, Innes trotting proudly at her mother's shoulder.

Because she was very young, we brought her on slowly and carefully. We gave her the winter off and the following March began riding her again.

Two months later, we took her to her first dressage competition. She was unfazed by the occasion and took a bold jump into the dazzling white competition arena. Her first dressage test score, of 62 per cent, reinforced our belief that she was bursting with talent and would go on to great things.

But that summer Innes suffered a broken leg when she panicked after being loaded into the trailer for a trip to Craven Country Ride. She kicked and crashed about in the confined space, rocking the trailer so hard it pushed forward the Land Rover it was attached to. Innes stopped after a couple of minutes and stood quietly, surrounded by pieces of smashed up metal partition. She had a nasty cut on her near hind leg and a deep puncture wound to the inside of her off-hind hock. The backs of her legs were badly scraped, suggesting she had fallen backwards in her frantic struggle to get out. Innes was led limping and bleeding on to the main yard. Her legs were bandaged and she was given antibiotics and painkillers. Vet Nick Johnson visited every day but Innes did not progress well. The wound over the hock joint was badly infected and wept yellow gunk. It was a horrible reminder of Alexander's nasty injury two years before. Innes hobbled along on the toe of the badly injured leg. She dragged herself about the box, not able to support any weight on it. Nick injected strong antibiotics and managed to clear up the infection. But Innes could still barely walk.

Jenny was terribly distressed. Her beautiful, athletic young mare was a cripple. Just days before, she had been bucking joyously round her large summer meadow. I had seen her mischievous sense of humour one sunny morning when I went up the field to check on her. Innes was lying down when I hove into sight. The naughty little horse, not wanting to be brought in, scrambled to her feet and ran off up the hill, looking back to see if I was following.

We were horrified to see that among the bits of wrecked trailer partition was a sheet of buckled metal with razor sharp edges. It was a miracle Innes had not sliced her legs to pieces as she thrashed about in a small space with that underneath her feet. The plastic-coated steel back bar, fastened behind her, was bent like a banana, and the back door of the trailer was almost kicked through.

Nick X-rayed the leg and discovered a chip of bone floating in it. Innes would have to go for an operation at Hird & Partners hospital.

Tim Booth, who had operated on Alexander, performed an MRI scan on Innes. It revealed a T-shaped fracture into the joint needing surgery to pin the bone together. It was a complex operation that involved inserting a screw into the leg through a small aperture, and there were no guarantees. But Tim was confident he could do it and said success would mean 'a gold standard repair for an athletic recovery.' Without surgery, Innes would quickly develop osteo-arthritis. The young horse would be an invalid, constantly in pain and with no viable future.

On Thursday, August 9, 2012, Tim and fellow surgeon Peter Schofield, who had just returned from veterinary duties with the equestrian team at the Olympic Games, operated on Innes. We could only hope the feisty little mare had inherited her mother's battling will to win. The day was traumatic. We were at work in Bradford, and Jenny sent out positive thoughts to Innes, mentally willing her to survive. The surgery was in the afternoon list and, as the interminable day dragged on, Jenny waited for the phone to ring. At 4pm, it did. But the call brought unwelcome news. Anaesthetist Sally told her Innes had not yet gone in for her operation. The two busy veterinary surgeons needed to get together for the complex procedure and final assessments were being made.

Our longest day just got longer.

At 7pm, Sally sent a text to say that all was going well in the operating theatre. Innes was still under, but not to worry.

Half an hour later, Sally rang.

"The operation is over and it has been a success," she said.

"Innes is on her feet. Her recovery from the anaesthetic was one of the quickest I have ever seen. She came round, blinked, shook her head and simply got up."

We visited Innes the next day. She had a giant bandage on and a drip in her neck. She had lost weight and looked the better for it. She perked up when she saw the apples we had brought.

That Sunday, there was a terrific storm over the hospital, similar to the one that heralded Innes's arrival, almost exactly a year before. The rain was torrential. Water welled up through the floor of the stable block and flowed in a stream down the centre aisle. The sky was black over the hills towards Halifax and lightning cracked across the sinister dark landscape. If it was a celebration of Innes's survival, it was certainly a spectacular one.

We visited Innes after work for the next few days. She made extremely good progress and was as bright as a button and full of her old mischief. She nudged off my flat cap, pulled up my coat to groom my back and made a mountain of her bed of fresh shavings.

A week after surgery, Innes was discharged from hospital. We could walk her a short distance to grass for four weeks, building up to longer walks during a further six weeks of box rest. We struggled to keep Innes quiet on her short walks. She had a wild look in her eyes and would sometimes buck and rear on the lunge line. I was in charge of walking duties and when she went up, I tried to stay calm, ignore it and keep her moving forward. It wasn't a lot different from handling Alexander's early tantrums in the school. Innes seemed to trust me and we fell into a routine. I loved our little walkabouts, even when they were a bit lively.

One night, as Christmas approached, Innes and I took a stroll in the moonlight. A single star shone above the dark hills and the stable yard glistened with a sheen of frost and ice. The little mare pattered along on her lead rope, her broken back leg now seemingly mended. Her unclipped winter coat was shaggy as a black bearskin rug and her unshod feet made little sound.

Three days after Christmas, Nick came to see Innes. Jenny turned her out in the school and she bucked round, flinging her heels high in the air. Then she settled into a purposeful extended trot around the perimeter fence. Nick passed her one hundred per cent sound, praising the brilliant surgeons who had screwed the bone back into place with such skill and precision that she floated over the ground in perfect rhythm and balance. Now she could be ridden again.

"You've got to be brave and start treating her just as a young horse, not a horse with a broken leg, because she isn't any more," Nick advised.

"Get on and ride her and, by the end of the summer, you should be competing together."

When the spring of 2013 came, and now recovered from my dressage accident, I began training Innes over the cross-country fences at home. She seemed tiny compared to the leggy height of Alexander, but she was well-rounded, with a strong bottom and a powerful neck, and I felt comfortable on her. She was a pocket rocket and we covered the ground as she skipped briskly along.

The training began on a warm April day. Innes and I set off up the hill in the cross-country meadow, passing sheep and lambs basking in the welcome sunshine. Innes was perky, but listening to me. Halfway up, I allowed her to trot. I felt her desire to go faster, but she kept it in check. We got three quarters of the way to the top and she could resist no longer. She broke into a canter and I went with her. She had behaved well and there was no point fighting her. We continued to canter along the top of the field, and for a moment I wondered when, or if, she would stop. But when I asked her, she pulled up. Soon after that, I jumped her for the first time when she towed me enthusiastically towards the little bank.

"All right, love. If that's what you want," I said, turning her to approach the obstacle.

Innes leapt confidently up on to the bank and unhesitatingly off the other side, tossing her head in excitement as she landed. Although she had not got Alexander's huge spring, she was bursting with energy and enthusiasm. We were beginning to gell and my confidence with her was building.

One fine evening in May, I rode her down the lane. I chatted away as usual, discussing the scenery and how pleasant it was to stroll along together. Innes didn't 'converse'like Alexander, whose big ears constantly go backwards and forwards as I rabbit away. She was too busy taking in her surroundings, often stopping to check out an interesting sight before bustling on again.

"Let's pop in here, love,"I said when our return journey brought us to the cross-country field.

The ewes and lambs had gone and the bottom gate stood invitingly open. We walked along the grassy path by the stream, rippling its way over its bed of ancient bricks and rocks to the pool beneath the willow tree. The meadow stretched enticingly ahead of us, bright with buttercups under the pale blue sky. Riding along on the little black mare in the peace and stillness of that spring evening, the pain and misery of winter seemed a lifetime away. Between us, we had been laid up injured for nine long months. It was as if we had both stepped out from the shade into the sun's renewing warmth.

Soon, Innes and I were galloping across the field. Running upwards together towards the deepening blue of the evening sky.

By the end of the summer we felt Innes was ready to tackle Camp Hill. She was now five years old.

I had decided to take her in the 65 cms class, while Jenny had steeled herself to ride Innes in the 50 cms.

When she was younger Jenny did not think twice about jumping fences over four feet high. In middle age, she had become very nervous about riding at all, and hardly ever jumped the smallest obstacle. But since Innes had come into her life she had dreamed of them leaping round a tiny course together to win a rosette.

As she waited nervously to start, Jenny got in a tangle tying her number. I quickly got permission for her not to wear it.

"But she has to wear her body protector. I can't allow her to go round without it,"said the lady at the start.

"I know it won't fasten,"said Jenny, struggling with the zip.

But it did. And then she was walking out on to the course. She and Innes were straight into their stride and leaping over the first obstacle. Jenny was transformed. The bundle of nerves on the verge of meltdown in the collecting ring was now the accomplished rider I knew so well. I followed them anxiously on foot, praying that all would go well. At last, they reached the final fence, the silver horseshoes. Innes soared over and the pair trotted through the finish flags.

I cheered and clapped and spontaneous applause broke out from the hill, where Eleanor Mercer was watching.

Jenny rode back to the collecting ring.

I dashed up and patted both horse and rider.

"You did it. You rode her so well,"I said.

"We got round,"Jenny replied. "It was a bit random. We were supposed to do it in trot, but it was a mixture of walk and canter. I don't think we'll get a rosette."

"The time looked pretty good to me,"I said. "I think you'll have done enough for a place."

I was right. Jenny finished second and soon appeared with her rosette, in pretty shades of green with gold stars.

"Isn't it beautiful?"she said, gazing at the colourful ribbon.

"We were told after Innes broke her leg that she would soon be leaping at the moon. Well, this is it."

I returned to the stables. Soon I would be riding Innes in a competition for the first time. The broken horse and the broken rider. As I was about to mount, I looked Innes in the eye. She stared back dispassionately, but there was a steely glint of determination. Already, she looked like a professional, ready to go out and do her job.

We walked down to the start.

"I'm far more worried about riding her than Alexander," I said.

I tightened the reins and Innes bounced forward keenly. We were soon at the first fence. I sat tight, anticipating the spring. It came but we were over nicely. Our first competitive fence. We were quickly over the second and the third. Innes was listening to me, easing back when I asked her to between fences. Three strides away from the next one, I let her take us in and over, then got her back again. We were in a good rhythm.

"Good girl, this is great fun,"I said.

Her ears were up. She was loving every moment.

Then we came to the skinny tyres. And, just like Alexander at the start of the summer, Innes refused to jump them. Three times I presented her at the skinny. Three times she refused it. But the fourth time I kicked her in and over she went.

Now we were bowling along again. Innes was flying everything out of stride. When we reached the silver barrels on the top of the hill, she took a great leap and I adopted the safety position.

"You were leaning back like Mary King!"Jenny said later.

We pinged the final horseshoes and crossed the finish line. Apart from the skinny tyres, we had jumped everything first time. I couldn't have asked for much more than that.

Sadly, there were no professional photos to mark Innes's first foray into the world of cross-country competing, but we were bolstered by the thought that there would be lots more opportunities.

How tragically wrong we were.

On the morning of Wednesday, October 16, 2013, I watched

Innes galloping and bucking round the field after I turned her out.

The following evening when I brought her in for the night, she refused the extra strong mint I always offered before buckling on her head collar. I led her on to the washing slats and told Jenny: "She didn't want her mint but I'm sure she's fine."

Jenny was immediately concerned. When she led Innes back into her stable, the little mare tried to roll. Something was clearly wrong. Jenny called the vet and began leading Innes round. If she was suffering from colic she must not be allowed to go down and risk a twisted gut. That could prove fatal.

Vet Helen Mottram was quickly with us and treated Innes for colic. Jenny returned to check on her horse at 10pm and 1am. There was a full moon. It was eerily silent and the bright moonlight cast long black shadows across the stable yard. Innes looked relaxed and comfortable. But by morning she had not done a poo and was showing no interest in the small haynet we had left her overnight. Helen came out again and Innes was given more treatment and time to recover. She was not showing any of the distressing symptoms of colic - sweating or kicking at her stomach. She was quiet and very tired. By lunchtime, Helen decided to refer Innes to the Philip Leverhulme Equine Hospital, near Chester. The renowned medical centre is part of the University of Liverpool and many colic cases go there to be treated. Jenny was by now tearful and very frightened.

Specialist horse transporter David Heap was contacted to take Innes to hospital. He set off from his stables at Burnley and soon his bright red horse wagon pulled up. It was side-loading, with a shallow, inviting ramp. There were windows all round and thick rubber matting right up the inside. CCTV cameras gave the driver a view of the horse passenger at all times.

Even in her distress, Jenny could not help admiring the

beautiful, compact little wagon, carefully designed for maximum comfort and safety.

Innes was sedated and her legs bandaged for the journey. A friend from the stables drove Jenny to the hospital, following the speedy little scarlet wagon as it made its way through Colne and along busy rain-soaked motorways towards North Wales. At the end of the M56, the wagon turned right and was soon pulling through the gates to the equine hospital.

Innes was expected and staff were immediately on hand. Her black coat dripped with sweat under her purple rug as she was led into the main treatment building. Up to fifteen vets, technicians and students were there to assess the emergency patient. But first she had to be persuaded into a padded metal stall in the middle of the big room. It took much coaxing, shoving and tugging. Her eyes rolled and she lashed out with her back leg, striking the scanning machine with a mighty metallic crash.

Jenny could only look on as the army of experts got to work, diagnosing and assessing. Her little mare had a tube up her nose, an arm up her bottom and a mass of high-tech equipment all round her. It was decided she needed emergency surgery. It would take up to two hours. The hospital would then ring Jenny. It was now after 5pm, dark and still pouring down. Whether the news was good or bad, there was little point in an interminable and terrible wait at the hospital. She and her friend set off back up the M6, now even more jammed with traffic. To Jenny, the crowded, rain-lashed motorway, with its glaring lights and swishing tyres, was a vision of hell.

She thought of the words of Karen Conroy, who bred Innes. "You love her too much."

Jenny was back home when her phone rang. She was by now in shock and misery and too afraid to handle the call. I took it and the news was bad. There was no impaction in the small intestine. The vet strongly suspected Innes had grass sickness. Only a biopsy would confirm that. Innes was comfortable and we would have to wait.

If it was acute grass sickness, there was no hope. It is the diagnosis we all dread. It causes a paralysis of the gut and is incurable. Even the wonderful vets at the hospital could not work miracles. If the biopsy showed it was grass sickness our gorgeous, talented, fun-loving little mare was doomed.

And so the waiting began. We were into the weekend and the result did not come through until late Monday afternoon. It was the start of a week off work that we had been looking forward to for months. A time to be together with our horses.

Our holiday had turned into a hell on earth. We were numb with grief and, in our hearts, we believed Innes was lost to us. Claire, one of the resident vets at the hospital, kept us fully appraised of her condition. Innes was comfortable and going for walks. There was still a faint glimmer of hope.

On Monday afternoon, we were told the biopsy result was inconclusive.

Another twenty four hours of waiting began. By Tuesday lunchtime, we could bear it no longer and headed off to the hospital. We would get there just about the time the second biopsy result was known. We arrived at 5pm and sat in the waiting room until Claire arrived. Our worst suspicions – what we had known in our hearts for four days - were confirmed. Innes had grass sickness.

We walked with heavy hearts to the intensive care unit to say goodbye.

Innes looked very quiet, very furry and very small on her immaculate bed of shavings. She had a large bandage round her tummy and spiralling white wires led up from her neck to a cluster of large drip bags. Her shoes had been removed before the operation and her winter coat was coming through. She looked very different.

When Jenny called her name, her ears twitched and her eyes brightened. We stroked and kissed her.

"Why couldn't you get better?"Jenny asked her.

Innes, kept comfortable on painkillers, yawned and her head drooped.

She was ready for a long sleep.

When I walked up to her, she nuzzled my pockets.

"Can she have a mint?"I asked Claire.

"No,"said Jenny. "You'll make her ill."

But she was ill. She was dying.

"Yes, she can,"Claire said.

The little mare took the mint and slowly savoured it. Her terrible sickness had started when she refused my mint five days ago. Now, at the end, she accepted it.

"I'm so proud of you,"I told her.

Then we left Claire to put her gently to sleep. She told us later how Innes was led out to the field and allowed to have a last nibble of grass – which could no longer harm her – before her peaceful death.

One of our worst nightmares – losing one of our horses – had just become a reality.

We drove home. Our route took us past the livery yard. It was a black night with a sprinkling of stars but no moon. Alexander put his head over the door and weaved it to and fro in excitement when he spotted Mum and Dad making a late visit. A friend had given him his tea, skipped him out and filled his haynet – and given him a cuddle from us.

Jenny's eyes were sore from grief. A dagger of ice had been thrust into her heart and she was sick to her stomach. The song: "How do I live?"kept running through her pain-numbed brain. It felt like there was nothing left.

Alexander continued to weave, and then he let out a loud

neigh. Jenny reached out to stroke his long, orange neck. He had never been her favourite, but his big light brown eyes glowed with affection.

Jenny felt a sudden upsurge of love for the tall ex-steeplechaser.

"It's just me and Steve now...and you,"she told him.

"And when the moon comes out, Innes will be leaping over it."

Jenny and Innes at Camp Hill

Chapter Sixteen

Goodbyes And Hellos

The tragic death of Innes left us with only one horse, Alexander.

The year before, we had allowed Daniel to move to a permanent loan home. It was a tough decision, driven solely by economic need. Money worries had haunted us for years and forced us to make some painful sacrifices. This one hurt the most.

Jenny and I tried to be sensible with our finances. But keeping the horses meant we were always short of money, no matter how much we cut back. Years ago, I gave up smoking to pay for Daniel's upkeep. I couldn't afford both, so the fags went overnight.

By January 2012, we had come to the end of the line trying to keep three horses. We did not want to sell any of them but we had to find a loan home for one, and we felt it had to be Daniel. He was by then nine years old, a mature horse who had found his feet, partly through the toughness of his character and also through the care and love we had lavished on him. He was at peace with the world and able to deal with any little problem it might throw at him. As long as he had a cosy bed, lots of attention and, most importantly, plenty to eat, he was happy. We also wanted to cut back on Daniel's competing. He had done incredibly well to achieve what he had in showjumping and cross-country events, considering that he was bred to pull carts rather than jump fences. We wanted him to live a long and happy life and easing back on his jumping, to look after his back and legs, would help him to do that. A home with someone who just wanted to hack out or ride in the school would suit him fine.

We advertised on the Horsemart website for a loan home for Daniel. Katie Mills, who lives in North Wales, was the first person to contact us and our instincts told us to look no further. It was clear from Katie's detailed email that her family gave their hearts and souls to their horses and would look after Daniel for all of his life. They came to see him and as we all stood in front of his box, he shot me an accusing look. Don't ask me how, but he knew why they were there. I could see him assessing his visitors. I could also see he approved of them. At the same time, the family had immediately taken to him. He was going to live far away but we knew he would be in loving hands. Katie would return in three weeks to take Daniel to his new home. It was a precious interlude.

The day Daniel left us, in the ultimate cost-cutting measure, was one of the most heartbreaking of my life. I had such a special bond with him. He has such a huge character, you can almost be tricked into thinking he is human. He is remarkably intelligent and perceptive, with a wicked sense of humour. There was a merry twinkle in his eye when we played our silly games, like head to head wrestling - those eyes, so deep and so much going on behind them. And never missing anything. He knows just what you are thinking at any given moment. As he instantly knew when he was to leave us.

As we waited for Katie and her family to arrive, Jenny kept her mind occupied by busying herself with Daniel's packing. I had to be with him in his stable. I brushed him endlessly and combed his tail and mane until they were as perfect as they could be. When there was no more brushing and combing to be done, I put my arm round his neck and chatted to him. He put his head down next to mine and I told him he was going on a long holiday with some lovely people who would give him everything he wanted, but if he got bored he could home at any time. I tried not to show I was upset, but he knew, and he suspected this was to be the day. His suspicions were confirmed when he caught sight of his travel boots waiting ready, inside his yellow feed bucket. I saw the look of realisation in his eyes and then a sadness. He nudged me gently and I hugged him again. The tears were close now. This was every bit as hard as I thought it would be.

And then the family arrived and they were as lovely as ever and we embraced. They went into Daniel's stable to make a fuss of him. His ears went back as he made a final appraisal. Then they came forward, his eyes softened and I could see he was ready to go with them.

Jenny dressed Daniel in his boots and travel coat. I went to check on something and when I returned to his stable, he wasn't in it. I dashed out of the barn and looked across to the trailer park. Daniel was standing there ready for loading, with the ladies all around him. He was gazing in my direction, as if searching for me. I rushed over and patted his neck and then I stepped away. It was time to hand him over. As the back door of the trailer was secured behind him, I spoke a few words of reassurance. Hearing my voice he craned his neck in a bid to look back at me. And then the trailer started to move, taking Daniel on a journey to a new life. As it turned out of the wagon park we heard a long, shuddering neigh.

We watched him being hauled up the hill one last time. As he went he let out another bellowing neigh. Daniel was waving goodbye. It was heartbreaking and the tears were now flowing. I peered through them until Daniel had disappeared from sight. I watched long after he had gone and then slowly turned away and trudged back to the yard.

That was more than five years ago and Daniel is now fifteen years old. We try to visit him every year and it is always a joy to see him. Katie regularly puts photos of him on Facebook and tells us how wonderful he is with her three young sons. Daniel has the perfect home and is as happy as a horse could be, but at the time it was so very hard to let him go.

Innes's death the following year left Jenny in a pit of despair that at times threatened to engulf her. A visit to Ian and Karen was about the only thing she could look forward to in those dark days. It felt almost as if we were coming home when we pulled up the winding drive to the stud farm. It was where Innes was born and Jenny took some comfort from being close to where her beloved little mare was raised, in the meadows above Grange-over-Sands, overlooking the magnificent Morecambe Bay estuary. In those gloomy winter days, the waters foamed murky brown under dark skies. But the view, always fascinating, endless and uncompromising, suited Jenny's raw pain and grief. She would stand gazing out across the bay, with its perilous quicksands and sucking currents under frothing waves and a vast expanse of ever-changing sky.

It was on one such visit that Karen suggested we took a look at a second of her home bred mares. When Jenny first saw the three-year-old Innes, another young horse was prancing about behind her in the field. The showy bay filly, with three white socks, was just two years old and sired by the dressage stallion, Demonstrator. She was called Dixie.

Jenny was instantly entranced by the little black mare standing at the gate, and Innes soon became the focus of all her hopes and dreams. But she could not help but admire the floating action and stunning deer-like face of the bay filly, and over the next two years Dixie trotted around on the edge of our story.

At this time, Karen had sent Dixie to a friend, Sarah Light, in Staffordshire to back and bring on.

"She's a sweet-natured, gentle horse and she will have lots of ability," Karen told Jenny.

"Why don't you go and visit her and see what you think?"

Jenny was unsure. She was bereft without Innes and didn't want to insult her memory by getting another horse too soon. On the other hand, it would give her hope and a purpose, another four-legged girl to devote herself to.

Although nothing could ever replace Innes, I was anxious that Jenny should find another horse, and I was convinced Dixie was the right choice. She was a lovely young mare from an impeccable background, with her whole future ahead of her.

"Dixie would give you something to plan for and look forward to through the winter," I said. "And to love and care for when a new spring finally comes."

We set out for Staffordshire in our little car, armed with no more than vague directions and a battered old map book. We guessed the journey would take around three hours and we expected to arrive by late lunchtime. The route was familiar for much of the way. We headed across to the M6 and then south down the motorway, passing the turn off, on the Cheshire/ Shropshire border, to the Somerford Park horse camps.

We made good progress and Jenny began to examine the map. There was a big problem with our atlas. It was at least twenty years old, and the ancient pages were so worn and creased that vital destinations were hidden in the folds. It was a Sunday but the motorway was busy and I had to keep my wits about me, while trying to discuss with Jenny the best place to exit. There were two options. One was to approach from the north, skirting round Stoke and travelling some distance, mainly on A roads. The alternative was to go south of our destination, but much closer to it, and cut across on minor roads, enjoying the pretty Staffordshire countryside. We chose the latter.

"Are you sure you know where you are going?" Jenny asked for the third time.

"Yes, yes. But you're the navigator. You follow the map."

It wasn't long before we realised we had left the road we were meant to be on and gone in a big loop. I pulled over and took hold of the atlas.

"Right," I said, decisively. "I think I see where we are. If we turn right just up ahead and follow that road for a bit, we can cut across east to where Dixie is."

We drove on uncertainly as the way became less clear. Time was passing and the light was already fading in the dank winter gloom of what was by now mid-afternoon. When I stopped at an unsigned junction of narrow country lanes our tempers began to fray.

"What do you think – left or right?" I asked.

"God knows," replied Jenny, getting crosser. "I've no idea where we are. It will be too dark to see Dixie by the time we arrive."

"Don't be ridiculous," I snapped, plunging the car down a narrow lane to the right. "We're almost there."

"You said that ten minutes ago."

We continued along the winding rural lane, the light still fading. I prayed we would not meet an oncoming vehicle as it was only wide enough for one car. We knew we were off the beaten track when we saw grass growing down the middle of the road. Even my optimism was waning, when we suddenly came to a junction.

"This is it," I said. "We go right here."

Two minutes later we passed the sign telling us we had

reached the hamlet of Blithbury and at the next corner we found the turn to Priory Farm Stud. A rutted, winding track led us between woods and fields until we reached the historic brick farm buildings.

The gloom had lifted a little and we could see an imposing farmhouse and adjoining stables. Exotic ducks and geese were swimming in a deep ford that formed part of a rushing stream passing in front of rich meadowland.

Sarah Light and her family welcomed us warmly into their country home. The traditional farmhouse dining room was dominated by a huge wooden table and there were many photographs of leaping horses on the walls. I was drawn to one in particular, of a bay horse jumping a huge hedge.

"Good grief! Who's that?" I exclaimed.

"That's me," said Sarah. "The mare is an ex-racehorse I got from Karen and Ian. I retrained her to do team chasing. She's got quite a jump."

"I can see that!" I said.

"We've got a lot of ex-racers from Karen and Ian, and from the trainer Martin Todhunter up in Cumbria," Sarah explained. "Some are out in the field with Dixie. Shall we stroll up?"

Walking to Dixie's field meant wading across the tree-lined ford, pretty as a picture book with its wonderful array of plumed and paddling waterfowl.

"Keep towards the side and you'll be fine," Sarah advised.

We had sensibly put on our long boots, which proved invaluable as the surging water came up to our calves. Soon we were safely across and heading over the soft, rain-sodden fields towards Dixie's lush and sheltered paddock. As we neared the gate I felt a nervous excitement in my stomach. I had not met Dixie before but I knew enough about her to want her to be part of our family.

Sarah opened the gate and we stepped into the field. Half a

dozen horses were grazing together in the middle. One of them glanced up, ears pricked, and then detached itself from the herd and trotted towards us. It was Dixie. She pulled up in front of us and looked at us expectantly. Her thick winter coat was plastered in mud and her feet were unshod. She was obviously enjoying her time out in the field. Her friends came running up to see what was going on. Jenny, always nervous around loose horses, retreated to the cover of the hedge as the herd circled us inquisitively. I was in my element as the thoroughbreds nudged and nuzzled me. Even caked in mud, they looked quality animals. They just hadn't made the grade as racehorses. Dixie followed me with her eyes as I went from one to another.

"Martin Todhunter sends me a few horses to look after and re-home," said Sarah.

"They are lovely natured and sweet as lambs most of the time - but some of them can be pretty lethal when you get on them!" she laughed.

As the friendly group of ex-racers milled around me, Dixie stood back, watching intently. She seemed to be willing me to go to her and when I did, she rested her head on my chest, trusting me. I tickled her chin affectionately and gave her a mint.

"We'll take her back to the yard and you can see her walking out and trotting," said Sarah, putting a head collar on Dixie. The mare walked quietly across the muddy fields and splashed without hesitation through the ford to the stable yard.

Jenny watched as Dixie was trotted up and down, displaying the same fine, floating action she had witnessed more than two years ago. She was a splendid looking creature, with a beautiful head and a deer-like grace. She was considerably bigger than Innes, being comfortably over sixteen hands high, with a broad, solid back.

Sarah assured us: "She is sweet and gentle. She was very easy to back and she has shown no reluctance or ill-will about being hacked out or ridden in the school."

To demonstrate, she led Dixie into the all-weather arena and ran alongside her as she hopped over a small cross-pole fence a couple of times.

"She's not worried at all," said Jenny.

"Nothing seems to bother her. She's just a really laid-back horse," Sarah replied.

"She's lovely," I said.

Jenny nodded her agreement.

It was time for us to go. We watched as Dixie was led across the ford in the thickening twilight to rejoin her friends in the field. Dusk was falling as we left the picturesque house and stables and set off on the long journey home.

I was certain that Dixie had chosen us. I felt an instant affinity with the big, sweet-natured mare and firmly believed she was destined to be part of our family. The way she had trotted so keenly up to us, and then refused to let go, reminded me of when Innes came running up the field at Grange-over-Sands that first time. In her quieter, less assertive way, Dixie too seemed to be saying to us: "Take me."

Over the next few days we talked a lot about Dixie. Her gentle nature had captured our hearts, but there was a snag. She had a number of sarcoids. These are unsightly wart-like growths that young horses can be prone to developing, and occasionally they are cancerous. One of Dixie's sarcoids was in a particularly tricky place, at the side of her wither – just where the front of a saddle would go. Many people are unwilling to take on a horse with sarcoids but both Alexander and the black mare, Dark Autumn, had them when they were youngsters. They had been successfully treated with a specialist veterinary ointment known as 'Liverpool cream'. Neither horse has been troubled by sarcoids since. Because our experience of treating sarcoids was so successful, we were not going to reject Dixie because of them. But, after Jenny's all-too recent heartbreak over Innes, she asked for a biopsy to ensure none of Dixie's sarcoids were cancerous. When the all-clear came from Staffordshire, Jenny made excited plans to transport Dixie to Yorkshire. She would be brought by David Heap, whose safe and speedy red horse wagon had taken Innes to hospital.

It was a stormy afternoon in early February when Dixie arrived. The rain lashed and the wind blew. She emerged from the little red wagon and looked around wondrously, before walking obediently into her carefully prepared stable, with its luxurious straw bed, well stuffed haynet and brimming pink water bucket.

Dixie was a lovely rich, dark bay colour, rather like a conker, with three white socks and a splash of white on her forehead. Her black mane was long, thick and straggly and her winter coat was like a dense, mahogany-coloured fur rug. She was tall and slender-legged with a huge shoulder and a compact but powerful body. Her quality was obvious, even with a big belly from her lazy winter. In temperament, Dixie was not at all like Innes. She was timid and cautious and her foal-like face peeped at us from the back of the stable. But she was gentle and trusting, and soon accepting carrots from Jenny's outstretched hand and starting to nibble at her haynet.

"You're going to love living with us," I told her, stroking her neck.

She looked round at me with her soft, doe-like eyes and allowed me to continue stroking her.

When I brought in a fork and bucket to skip out the stable, she turned round and joined me, watching what I was doing and nudging the fork handle, as if offering to help. It was clear she loved people and wanted to interact.

The plan was to allow her to settle in for a few weeks, while the sarcoids were treated, and then start bringing her back into work. She had at least six sarcoids. There was one on the front of her chest, two on the outside of her near hind leg, an ugly-looking one on the inside of the same leg and another under her tummy. But by far the most concerning was the one on the side of her wither.

Vet Nick Johnson examined it and his verdict was a terrible blow.

"The roots could be deep and widespread. When it is treated, the area affected is going to be very large. This is going to take months, rather than weeks to heal. Even then, we will have to see if the skin is strong enough to take a saddle. It is just possible she may never be able to be ridden."

Jenny rang Karen with the devastating news.

"We'll come and fetch her," Karen said. "There's no point you paying to keep her there. We'll get our vet to treat her and she can spend a nice long summer with us. If all goes well and it has healed enough to take a saddle, we'll bring her back in October."

So, a week after her arrival, Dixie was loaded into Ian and Karen's trailer and in a couple of hours, she was enjoying the fresh sea air back at her birth place. Time is said to be a great healer and we trusted that would be the case.

Dixie was far too beautiful never to be ridden.

Jenny had not sat on a horse over the long, sad winter months since Innes died. With Dixie gone, she felt sure that unless she found a mount for the spring and summer, she would never ride again. She spent hours trawling equestrian websites for horses to loan or buy. She wanted something that was not too big, powerful or energetic. Something with a gentle nature that she could ride without worry and build her confidence on. And something that could then be returned to its owner, or easily sold on.

On February 18, 2014, we joined a one-day regional journalists'strike over the threat of redundancies. We are not hard core union people. In fact our membership of the National Union of Journalists was very hit and miss, but the livelihoods of colleagues were at stake so we kept away from the office. We could not face manning the picket line though and decided our time could more usefully be spent looking for a temporary replacement for Dixie.

Jenny got up early on the day of the strike and set about her website search with new energy. At first it was unpromising, but then she came upon a local site she had never seen before. She found herself staring at a bright-eyed bay mare called Sprite. She was said to be rising six years old and 15.2hh. The photograph showed her tied to a fence wearing what appeared to be a red harness, but Jenny was immediately struck by her alert expression. Her sparkling presence shone out from the computer screen. She had a look that suggested she was determined to go places.

Jenny was instantly bewitched.

"Let's go and see her," she urged.

Sprite lived at a small livery yard on a hillside farm overlooking Bradford. But Jenny's eager anticipation vanished when she set eyes on her. It was immediately apparent that the little mare was nowhere near 15.2hh. At a guess, she was barely 14.2 and very dainty, with tiny little hooves. Her owner, Shoulanne, was obviously very proud of her and had tied a red ribbon in her long dark mane especially for her visitors. We hadn't the heart to just walk away and so she was tacked up for us to try out.

Sprite was bred in nearby Brighouse as a 'fine road trotter' and had pulled a little cart round the centre of Halifax before

Shoulanne bought her. Since then she had just done a bit of hacking out. But though clearly green, Sprite's potential was soon obvious. She refused to stand still as I tried to get on, fretting and spinning while Jenny and Shoulanne struggled to hold her still. But when I did at last manage to slide into the tiny old-fashioned leather saddle, she did not object.

Although Sprite was by far the smallest horse I had ever ridden, I did not feel I was dwarfing her and she seemed to carry me easily. When we went into a small concrete yard and began to walk a circle, I instantly felt her athleticism. Her nervousness could not hide her enthusiasm. I talked quietly and encouragingly and she listened, both to my voice and my leg. And though it was clear she was not certain how to respond to my aids, she did her best to follow my instructions. She was willing to learn and was soon taking confidence from me, moving quickly off my leg as I made the most of our makeshift arena.

Sprite was again uncertain when it was time to go out on to the lane, but with more quiet words, a stroke of her neck and a firm shove with my lower leg and bottom, she was soon briskly on her way. Coming back, we trotted for the first time. It was effortless and springy. Sprite had a bounce and enthusiasm that brought back painfully raw memories of my rides out on Innes. Before leaving, we watched her being turned out. She scampered over the top of the thick mud in the gateway to join her friends in the big sloping field. As the little mare cut through the other horses, tossing her head and bucking, before rolling over and over in the mire, Jenny asked me: "Does she remind you of anybody?"

I did not need to answer.

That evening, Jenny texted Shoulanne to say that although Sprite was a lovely horse, she was too small for us. The next day, she changed her mind and asked if we could take another look at her.

Sprite was as bright and animated as the previous day. Her passport revealed that her proper name was Lady Spiritus and she was a year older than we had thought, rising seven. Jenny's mind was made up. Sprite had to be hers and she agreed to buy her for the £800 asking price.

Sprite arrived two days later. She settled in quickly and there was certainly more to her than first met the eye. She was bright as a button and neat as a new pin; full of zest, bounce and elasticity. Within days we were wondering just what we had bought. She was fascinated by everything and scarcely had time to snatch at her haynet or take a drink for fear of missing something. Although it was almost certainly her first time on a horse walker, Sprite marched round at the front, tossing her head, urging the roundabout-like contraption to spin faster. The second time she was put on it, there was a gelding in the metal compartment behind her. She turned to face him while the machine was revolving, walking effortlessly backwards for several strides, before spinning on a sixpence to face the right way again.

When Sprite wanted anything, she pawed the air with her front leg to attract attention. Seeing Jenny crossing the yard, she would insistently wave the leg while she was on the walker, stepping forward indignantly when the metal barrier bumped her bottom.

Within days, I was riding Sprite down the lane. It was early March and spring was just around the corner. The mild, wet winter was bringing up the new grass in the big pastures and the splendid show of snowdrops had given way to carpets of crocuses. The daffodils were in bud and we heard the woodpecker drumming in the thick belt of trees between the lane and the canal towpath. Sprite marched along, stopping abruptly now and again to take in the sights and smells of the countryside.

After two weeks, she was tearing round her field refusing to be caught. Even when it was emptied of the other mares, she proved elusive, running around for several minutes on her own before consenting to come in.

The small bay mare quickly carved out a special place in Jenny's heart. She was her beloved and pampered little pet, her 'dear Spritelet.' Innes's death had broken her heart, but a bright-eyed Bradford pony gave her life new purpose.

With Dixie at Ian and Karen's stud farm

Chapter Seventeen

Alexander's Great Escape

There were five weeks to the race and training was going well.

We had done fifteen circuits of the indoor school without stopping – the race distance of one and a quarter miles - and had upped our hill work to four trots and three canters in one session.

Alexander was back out in his field after Michael Bradley said he was happy with the leg wound. And Charles Barker had given the thoroughbred the all clear following a routine dental inspection. Alexander was also booked in for his annual back check. I felt we were doing everything possible to have him in top condition.

He was now wearing a new fly mask when he was ridden or turned out in the field. Alexander is terribly bothered by flies and also suffers from a summer allergy, made worse by pollen and sunlight. I decided it was time to get his mask back on when he started bouncing on the spot and throwing his head around to get rid of the flies at the end of an uphill canter session. I dismounted as a precaution and led him back to the yard. There was always a danger of having an accident during the race - I certainly didn't want one before it.

Sponsorship money continued to pour in. I had already raised what I needed to take part. The generosity of friends at the yard was humbling. Ten, twenty and even thirty pounds were being donated on an almost daily basis.

One day I found an envelope wedged in the bars of Alexander's stable. It was the bill from our farrier, Steven Hardaker. On the bottom of it Steven had written: "Less Alex front shoes, £37, re sponsorship form," with a smiley face.

Alexander was feeling fantastic. His cut leg had not set us back at all. He had bags of energy on our training runs and seemed to be finding the fast uphill work very easy. And yet he remained completely professional and I had total control.

Ian Conroy had warned that Alexander would get more lively the harder we worked. But so far it hadn't happened, even when I pressed the accelerator to the floor one day. I was itching to know how much petrol was in Alexander's tank. It would help me to plan the final weeks of our training. I chose to run him in one of our favourite fields. It had a gently sloping hill, perfect to test his stamina, and the ground was ideal, with just enough give in it.

We set off at a fast canter. Halfway up the hill I gave him a squeeze with my legs and he upped the tempo to a three-quarter gallop. He reached the top effortlessly and gradually pulled up to a bouncy stop.

We walked back down the hill, turned and set off again, this time at a gallop. Alexander was lobbing along happily, but I wanted him to go flat out. I crouched low over the saddle, gave him a kick and began throwing the reins at him. He responded, but I kept kicking and chucking the reins and made sure he galloped all the way to the top. As we pulled up he tossed his head in excitement. He was now breathing hard, but he seemed keen to do more.

I turned him and we walked down the hill again. Now Alexander was prancing and arching his neck excitedly. He was eager to run up the hill again, but he was still listening to me and he waited until I was ready before setting off.

We pelted up the hill three more times. After each run Alexander was puffing but he was quick to get his breath back. He had told me what I wanted to know. He had plenty of fuel in the tank.

I was further encouraged by the control I'd had. Alexander had done everything I asked of him and the flat out galloping had not blown his brains. If he was as well behaved on race day we would be all right.

I allowed myself a broad smile of contentment as we jogged back to the yard, and reflected on what a different horse Alexander had become. If I had galloped him like that a few years ago it might not have ended so happily. Anything could happen when he was young and unpredictable. I remembered only too well the time he got himself so wound up he escaped from me on the road. It was one of the most horrific days of my life.

It happened after I took him to the Christmas trail ride at Craven Country Ride in December 2013.

There was an edgy excitement about Alexander as Jenny got him ready that day. He looked very smart, although she stopped short of dressing him in the festive decorations many horses were sporting.

"I don't really think you're a red felt antlers person," she said, as Alexander paced round his stable, showing the whites of his eyes.

I hacked over with two teenagers from the yard. They were dressed as a zebra and a crocodile and their ponies were wreathed in red and green tinsel. When the Ride came into sight, Alexander realised where we were and stopped to survey the scene, ears pricked and body tense. He snorted excitedly.

He danced about as we waited at the start for the signal to set off. When it came, he charged off up the first steep hill, throwing himself sideways for a few strides. I legged him forward and he broke into a lovely fast canter, with me crouched like a jockey, the girls following on their ponies. We pulled up at the top of the hill and started to walk down the other side.

Alexander was keen to go again but I restrained him until we reached the next hill. The instant I relaxed the reins, he sprang forward powerfully and set off at a gallop. We hurtled to the top, where we pulled up, Alexander still bouncing and tossing his head. I was concerned that he might unsettle the ponies. It would be safer for the girls if we got out of their way.

"We'll go round on our own," I said. "We'll see you at the finish."

We trotted on ahead up the next hill and tiptoed down the steep descent on the other side. Now we had reached a wide flat meadow and Alexander needed no persuasion to gallop across it, coming back to a fast canter to go through the gateway, and cantering on down the hill through a water obstacle. After a few more canters and gallops, we reached the first line of jumps. Alexander leaped over them, towing me enthusiastically into everything I pointed him at.

Before we were halfway round the trail, he was white with sweat, mostly through sheer excitement. In what seemed no time at all, we reached the final hill and Alexander cantered down it, still full of energy and enthusiasm.

"Good grief! I'm glad it's you sitting on that and not me," exclaimed Jenny as Alexander bounced through the finish flags, his head shaking and his eyes rolling.

"That was brilliant," I said, jumping off.

Jenny led Alexander round in the unsaddling area. He was lathered in sweat and splattered with mud, but he was still keen and looked ready to go round again. There was no sign of the girls on their ponies and he was not settling.

"I'll ride back on my own to keep him moving," I said.

"Wait for the girls. You'll never manage all those gates," Jenny replied.

"We'll be all right. They're fairly straightforward."

Jenny was not convinced but I was anxious to stop Alexander getting more wired, so I remounted and set off.

Our route home involved opening and closing a series of ten gates before reaching the road between the villages of Gargrave and West Marton. Alexander was not good with gates when he was younger, though he is one of the best now, and though he stood still while I opened them, he then dashed through, and did not see the point of waiting for them to be closed.

We managed to get through most of the gates without incident.

"Good lad, you're doing well," I encouraged.

But then I had to deal with a particularly low catch and try as I might, I could not reach it.

"I'm sorry lad. I'm going to have to get off for this one."

I unhooked the gate, we walked through and I fastened it behind us. But getting back on proved problematic. Alexander would not stand still. Every time I stood on the gate and prepared to put my foot in the stirrup, he shuffled away out of reach. We to-ed and fro-ed for five minutes, then I tried standing on a pile of stones but they were too wobbly. We went back to the gate but he still refused to stay in the right place.

"For God's sake, Alexander! We're never going to get home if you keep buggering about!"

Finally, I got him to a grassy mound and while his attention was caught by a mouthful of grass, I got back on.

But I had to dismount again at the penultimate gate, and knowing the final one was awkward, I led him to that and walked him through it. Once it was fastened, I had the same rigmarole of trying to get back on, but this time we were on the road. Alexander would not stand side-on to the gate, insisting on turning to face it, or moving away. Another insecure pile of stones failed to work. After a further five or ten minutes we were both getting pretty fed up. At last I made him stand still, but he was a yard away from the gate.

"There's nothing else for it. Now don't move!" I shouted in frustration.

I perched on the gate, took the reins in my left hand and reached my left foot across towards the stirrup, intending to get it in and vault on.

But Alexander had had enough. He dashed forward. I quickly put my foot back down as he tried to set off. Desperately, I pulled back with the reins but his 'naughty head' was now in full control. He fought me, tugged his head away and broke into a canter, pulling me to the ground. For an instant I clung to the reins, but I knew he was not going to stop and I let go.

He set off down the road. I picked myself up. There was a big hole in the right knee of my jodhpurs and my knee was bleeding. But there was only one thought in my head.

"Alexander - stop!"I shouted after him, twice, pleading with him.

He peered round at me and slowed to a brisk trot – but kept going. He had decided he could make it home better on his own. What he didn't know was that he could meet a tractor, a milk tanker, or a bin wagon coming the other way. But I knew. And the image that sprang into my mind was a vision from hell.

"Alexander, stop – please," I called out again. This time he didn't turn round.

I tried desperately to run after him, but I was tired, fifty five years old, my knee hurt and my body protector was constricting my chest. All I could manage was a laboured jog.

I kept shouting after him but at the road junction, without hesitating, Alexander turned left and headed off towards Gargrave, and the yard, two miles away. He knew where he was going, but not the hazards he could face on the way. I could still see him but he was disappearing at a fast trot into the distance and I could not keep up. My lungs were bursting and I was forced to walk for a while, gasping for breath. Alexander had now gone from my sight, hidden in the folds of the road and the surrounding walls and trees. I had an awful sickly feeling in the pit of my stomach. I had never felt so helpless in my life. There was nothing I could do, except to begin another slow jog.

A cyclist suddenly came into view.

"My horse has got loose. Have you seen him?"

"Yes. I tried to stop him but he ran off from me."

"Oh my God!"

I jogged on until I reached a farm. I peered hopefully into the yard but there was no sign of Alexander.

Another cyclist rode up."My horse has run off. Could you try to catch him, please?"I pleaded.

"I'll see what I can do,"he said uncertainly and pedalled off.

I had started trudging up the hill on the other side of the farm when a car approached from behind. It was a smart saloon with a well-dressed, middle-aged couple in it. I stood in the middle of the road and waved it down with grim determination. I wasn't going to move. The car stopped. The man in the passenger seat wound down his window nervously.

"My haarse…"I began, in a whirl and breathless.I tried again."My horse has got away from me. He's heading that way. Would you help and give me a lift?"

God knows what the respectable couple thought as they observed this wild-eyed man with a hole in his trousers and a bloody knee. But to their credit, they did not hesitate.

"Get in the back. Watch out for the baby seat."

We drove up the hill and as we crested it, I saw a wonderful sight. A country chap, in his early thirties and wearing a flat cap, was walking towards us on the opposite side of the road. He was leading Alexander by his dangling reins.

"Oh, thank God, thank God! Please stop!"

I grabbed at the door handle but nothing happened. I couldn't get out.

"Hold on," said the man. "It's the child lock."

He got out of the car and freed me. I thanked the couple profusely. The cyclist was also in attendance. They all looked perplexed, including the chap holding Alexander. It seemed he was a local farmer. He was calm but looked relieved to see me. His smart Land Rover Defender was parked facing us a hundred yards further down the road. He must have got out and caught Alexander as he trotted over the hill.

I stroked Alexander's neck.

"You daft bugger. You gave me a terrible fright."

The relief was pouring out of me.

I thanked the farmer, who seemed to become more worried when I told him Alexander was an ex-racehorse who had got a bit excited going round the trail ride. We walked to a nearby gateway.

"What do you want me to do?" asked the farmer.

I clambered on to the gate.

"If you can keep him in, hold the stirrup and hold his head for me."

Alexander was a bit jumpy but I got on safely.

The farmer still looked anxious but I assured him: "He'll be all right now."

My gratitude and relief were beyond measure. I feared I would come across Alexander literally in pieces. It was a feeling of indescribable horror.

Two weeks later, Alexander spectacularly bucked me off in

the arena while indoor showjumping at Osbaldeston Riding Centre in Lancashire. It was my first fall since the horrendous dressage accident ten months before and it left me shaken, and with my confidence knocked.

We love Osbaldeston. In our first year of competing, Alexander and I qualified for the Trailblazers finals by jumping a double clear in the 75cms class there.

This time, my Osbaldeston experience was very different.

Alexander was twitchy in the collecting ring and seemed cross and disengaged. He was jumping with a huge spring and bounce and I was having to work hard to keep my balance. He got giddy and difficult to control in the 65cms jump off and a loss of concentration caused him to knock down two fences. The 75cms class was looking good until the third last fence when our stride was wrong. Alexander got right under it, coiled himself and really used his back end to propel us over. I rocked slightly as we landed but immediately got back into the driving seat, reining him in and right-legging him in line for the second last. He tried to dash off in another direction and we were wrong again at the fence. He twisted to launch us up and over and I lost my balance again. I fought to regain it but before I could recover, Alexander had thrown his toys out of the pram. Suddenly, I was on a bucking bronco.

"Stop, stop!" I shouted. But he wasn't listening.

I was launched, landing on my right side and banging my head. I lay winded, struggling to get my breath, as anxious organisers and spectators hurried to assist.

"Can you move your legs?" asked one.

I lay on my back waving them merrily like a stranded beetle.

Alexander had galloped off, bucking madly, to the arena exit gate.

Jenny headed into the ring to see if I was still alive. As she approached, I sat up.

"I'm all right," I assured her. "I'm just annoyed he bucked me off when we were clear with only one fence left to jump."

"Do you want me to take this anywhere?"asked a young man who had caught and was holding Alexander.

"The pie factory,"replied Jenny, her nerves in shreds.

Cantering Mister McGoldrick (courtesy of New Beginnings)

Chapter Eighteen

A Racing Legend And A Film Star

Over the years Alexander and I have formed a bond. We understand, respect, trust and care for each other. This togetherness has given us the confidence to tackle bigger and more technical cross-country courses. The rosettes we have won at hunter trials, one-day events and showjumping are testament to the absolute belief we have in each other and what we are doing. I hoped our partnership would carry us all the way when we got to the racecourse.

My confidence was given a boost in 2015 when I was allowed to ride the former racehorse Mister McGoldrick.

I had been reunited with him twelve months earlier at Skipton Races. I was walking round the course, examining the fences and still musing about whether I might be tempted to jump them, when I bumped into Keith Rosier.

"Have you seen your old mate?" he asked.

I looked at him, confused.

"Mister McGoldrick. I've warned them his stalker is here!" Keith smiled.

I completed my course walk with a big grin on my face and then set out to find the ex-racer. He was standing in a grassy area close to the parade ring and within a few strides of the winning post, with his handler, a calm and cheery man in his forties. 'Mac' was wearing a green rug emblazoned with his name and the words New Beginnings. The Yorkshire racing legend was clearly as popular as ever in retirement. Fans were milling around him, patting and stroking him and being photographed with him. As the next race began there was a lull in the stream of visitors and I pounced.

"Hello," I said to the man. "Am I all right to see him?"

"Of course. That's why he's here."

The man was Kevin Atkinson who runs the New Beginnings racehorse rehabilitation charity in North Yorkshire with Pam Hollingworth. They take in ex-racers, retrain them and find them suitable loan homes or care for them at their stables for the rest of their days. I was soon to learn of the wonderful work they do, inspiring me to try to help.

Then aged seventeen and retired for two and a half years, Mister McGoldrick was their ambassador, going to racecourses to raise their profile and encourage people to donate to the charity. Excitedly, I took my turn to pat and stroke him. I was so thrilled by the unexpected reunion I missed two of the races to spend time with my racing hero.

Mister McGoldrick had got quite excited during the first race but he soon relaxed and even looked as if he was nodding off at one point. But when the racehorses galloped past a few yards away his head came up and he watched them intently as they hurtled round the corner. There was a competitive look in his eye that said: "I could still do that - and I'd beat you!"

Kevin said Mister McGoldrick was ridden every day, and although he still pulled strongly, he was very well-behaved. He was being schooled to do Retraining of Racehorses showing classes.

Kevin explained: "We take our time with the horses. We leave them in the field to chill out, and to get racing out of their system, for as long as it takes.

"When we do start to work them again we use long reins

before they are ridden. You have to take your time. The worst thing you can do is go too quickly with them."

His words struck a chord. There was no doubt that some of the falls I'd had from Alexander over the years were down to me trying to run before I could walk.

The following summer, Jenny and I went to visit Kevin, Pam and the New Beginnings horses. We had seen them a couple of months earlier at the Middleham racing stables open day in North Yorkshire. Mister McGoldrick was guest of honour at one of the yards and looked fantastically well as I chatted in the sun with Kevin and Pam. We had become friends after I had raised £200 for the charity with the horse calendar. Mister McGoldrick featured as Mr July and was present when I handed over the money.

During our conversation at Middleham, the possibility of me riding Mister McGoldrick was mentioned. Although 'Mac' is ridden by a New Beginnings volunteer at racecourse parades, and by Pam at home, he is not a riding horse for the general public. But Kevin and Pam were grateful for my fundraising efforts and for publicity I provided with a magazine feature about Mac and his new life with the charity, and they wanted to say thank you.

I did not really believe it would happen, until I sent Kevin a Facebook message the evening before our visit and he replied: "Don't forget your riding hat."

The day of our trip to the charity dawned bright and sunny. The New Beginnings horses grazed and swished contentedly in their big meadows, tucked away in picturesque rolling countryside down a gated lane. We sat and chatted with our friends over coffee and biscuits, until Pam suddenly said: "So, Mister McGoldrick. Do you want to ride him?"

"Well, yes," I replied, feeling desperately nervous now the magical moment had arrived. Here was a once in a lifetime opportunity to ride a steeplechasing star who had finished third in the Queen Mother Champion Chase at the Cheltenham Festival, beating Moscow Flyer and Kauto Star. I felt proud and privileged that I was trusted to ride him.

Pam brought Mac out of his field and handed me his lead rope. I tried to look nonchalant but I felt far from it. Mac was quiet and relaxed and I stroked his nose and patted his neck. I led him into his stable, with a great open view of the meadows below, and Kevin and Pam tacked him up. He turned to snap his teeth, like Alexander does, as he was girthed, but otherwise was placid. He had on a brown snaffle bridle and a running martingale, the same type of bridle he wore when racing.

I led him into the outdoor arena. Now it was happening, the nerves faded and I began to enjoy myself. Pam held Mac as I got on to the mounting block, took hold of the reins and swung my leg across his back. And suddenly I was sitting on him, and grinning like the Cheshire Cat!

We began to walk around the arena. Mac was positive and it felt very natural. I tried to focus on riding him like any other horse, and we seemed to gel. I felt relaxed and so did he, but it was such a thrill. I changed the rein and started to turn him in smaller circles, seeing if he moved off my leg. He was very responsive. Then Pam said I could trot him. He moved beautifully into the trot, and flowed along, very forward but relaxed and rhythmical. It was lovely. Again, I changed the rein and made smaller circles.

Suddenly Pam said: "Canter him when you're ready, Steve."

This was a huge surprise. I did not expect to be allowed to canter him. I gathered myself together for a few yards and then asked. Mac instantly moved into a wonderful forward-going, balanced canter. He had a gorgeous rhythm and we swept round the arena three or four times before Kevin told me to bring him back because he was getting a bit warm in the heat. We eased back to trot and then walked for a few minutes more before we decided he had done enough. I stayed on him while some last photos were taken and then finally got off. I had ridden him for about twenty minutes and it had been amazing.

I led Mac back to his stable and watched him for a few minutes as he tucked into his hay. It had been an honour to ride him and everything I could have dreamed of. At the age of eighteen, he was in tip-top condition and had given me one of the most thrilling experiences of my life.

Meanwhile, I had a decent 2015 with my own former racehorse. Alexander had been brilliant during the winter indoor showjumping season, leaping 168 fences in competition without knocking a single one down, and we again qualified for the Trailblazers finals.

We warmed up for the outdoor season with a cross-country lesson at Camp Hill with Eleanor Mercer who had us working hard on the technical stuff. She described Alexander as clever and genuine.

It set us up nicely for the Mini Hunter Trials series, and during the summer I reached new heights by jumping a 3ft 9ins fence, as well as a daunting 3ft 6ins-high brush fence, with a three-foot-wide open ditch in front of it. Our consistent efforts bagged us third place in the 65cms series and we ended our season at Camp Hill by competing in the 80cms class at the one day event. I had just a couple of weeks to learn the dressage test, but it was straightforward. I was confident we could do an accurate test, but probably not much more than that.

It was hot and sunny at the event, the worst kind of weather for Alexander's summer allergy. It had become so bad that his twitching and head-shaking meant he had to wear a zebra print fly mask all the time he was not actually competing. We whipped it off seconds before he set out on the cross-country course or entered the showjumping ring. He also wore crocheted blue 'ears' and we smeared Vaseline in his nose to try to stop pollen getting up it.

The dressage test was in a pretty meadow near to a group of trees. It may have been the pollen, or the flies, but Alexander became distressed and agitated as we warmed up. We entered the arena in bounce and he continued to chuck himself around while I defied the rules by whispering reassurance to him from the corner of my mouth. Despite that, we managed a tidy test, though his unsettled behaviour certainly cost us marks. I gave a flourishing salute and a beaming smile at the end, and the lady judges laughed as Jenny told me off for leaving the arena quickly by the most direct route, straight out the side!

Our dressage score was 39.5, which left us down at the bottom end of the field of 28. We got nice judges' comments, including 'super rhythm,' 'very well ridden' and 'lovely horse' and I got a mark of seven for my riding, which I was pleased with. But we were out of contention for a place, so I set out to enjoy the two jumping phases.

Our showjumping round was out of the top drawer. It was a lovely big grassy arena and we got into a nice rhythm. Alexander didn't touch a pole as we went clear.

Then it was the cross-country. The only fence that bothered me was the Spider, a narrow obstacle with black twisted legs, which Alexander was not comfortable with. But I followed Eleanor's advice, bringing him back and setting him up for it, then squeezing him on two strides out, and he jumped it without hesitation. Our technical lesson at the start of the season paid off when we successfully negotiated a tricky three fence combination. We were clear again to finish on our dressage score. Frustratingly, our final position was 11th, one place and half a point out of the rosettes, but I was thrilled with the way we had jumped.

A few weeks later I got a huge surprise. We arrived home after a long and tiring day at work in Bradford to find a parcel propped up against the back door. Inside was a silver trophy and a pretty rosette. With them was a note, written by Eleanor Mercer's mum, Fran. It read: "The Camp Hill Challenge Trophy is awarded by Eleanor for the best or most improved riding of the day and this year she would like it to go to Steve and Alexander for their excellent double clear!"

It was for our showjumping and cross-country rounds at the one day event. I was gobsmacked. My riding had been recognised by a professional event rider. It showed how far I had come.

Jenny took a photo of me with the trophy and rosette and put it on Facebook. I was humbled by the good wishes of friends at the yard, other equestrians, work colleagues and family, saying the award was well deserved.

But I couldn't have done it without my wonderful horse.

Alexander's adventures in 2015 were not confined to his competing. For the second time in his life, he was a photographic star.

During the summer I was contacted by social photographer Red Saunders to assist him in his latest work. We had helped Red four years earlier when he needed a pair of horses for a living tableau of an English Civil War scene. We agreed to take Alexander and Daniel to a remote location in Bronte Country for the photographic shoot on a blisteringly hot day in July 2011. It had its challenges but the fact that we were being paid £200 convinced us it was worth doing.

As Jenny said: "It pays the electricity bill."

We reached our destination along a narrow lane that in many places wasn't wide enough for two vehicles to pass. It wound through tiny hamlets and plunged up and down frighteningly steep hills, but at last we passed a remote reservoir and reached our turn-off. The farm track was narrow and went over a tiny stone bridge, before bending immediately sharp right into a steep, uphill climb, surrounded by high grassy banks and grazing sheep.

It took ten minutes of anxious manoeuvring to get the trailer up the incline. With enormous relief we reached the top and parked in the large field in front of the farmhouse that was being used as a studio.

The views were breathtaking, sweeping miles over the valley to further hills and isolated farmsteads. In the distance tiny horses, cattle and sheep cropped the upland pasture, like plastic miniatures on a model railway board. The sun beat down, turning the spectacular scenery into a shimmering mirage.

More than forty local people, dressed in period costume, were involved in the photo shoot. Alexander was to be the horse of the captain of the soldiers. Originally, an 'extra' in full regalia was lined up to sit on him but we were extremely worried about that arrangement. It was someone who couldn't ride, let alone handle an unpredictable thoroughbred. The organisers saw the sense of what we were saying and asked me to take the captain's part. I was ushered into the temporary costume and make-up room to be transformed into a Cromwellian cavalry officer. I emerged in thigh-high leather boots and spurs, with metal gauntlets over my hands and a feathered hat. Sophie was invited to feature as a soldier.

The next step was to get on Alexander while wearing my heavy, clanking captain's regalia. Daniel had already taken the sight of a blacked-up, metal-helmeted Sophie in his stride. The grass was lush and he carried on munching.

Alexander was equally, though more unexpectedly, good natured as I levered myself on board from a raised rocky outpost. As a final flourish, I was furnished with a long iron sword, that was fastened around my waist and left to dangle down Alexander's side.

Guides led us back down to the stone bridge and along a tree-lined path and then a narrow road to the film location. It was further than we expected but finally we wended our way through a wood and emerged above a clearing, where we could see Red and his entourage waiting below in an historic battle camp scene. We picked our way carefully down a steep grassy path to the dell. We were roasting in our outfits and the horses were plagued by swarms of flies. They were to be photographed individually, and separately from the other people in the tableau. Red would use his expertise to put the scene together later.

Sophie's role was to stand with Daniel as he grazed. He was happy to be filmed, only becoming bored after his moment of fame had passed. While waiting for Alexander, he broke free from Sophie and legged it back along the narrow grassy path to the camp site.

My task was more testing. Mounted on Alexander, I had to stand in the middle of the clearing in front of a large blue screen while Red and his many disciples clicked away, only breaking off for film extras to rearrange our position and fiddle about with the sword. One particularly enthusiastic production woman fussed around us, repeatedly moving the sword. The session seemed to go on forever and I could feel that Alexander was becoming concerned. His composure had been amazing considering he was hemmed in by people, cameras were flashing and clicking from all angles and the big blue screen loomed over him. To make matters worse, the sword was slipping and rubbing down his flank. He began twitching and prancing as more adjustments were made and more shots were taken. I sat quietly in the burning heat, talking to him and keeping the reins as loose as I dared. The production crew was oblivious to the danger that was building. If Alexander lost it, people could be knocked over and injured and thousands of pounds worth of photographic equipment wrecked in seconds.

Jenny, watching in terror from the edge of the film set, said afterwards she felt physically sick waiting for Alexander to explode. To his eternal credit he stayed in control and the completed artwork shows a relaxed horse and rider.

When we eventually arrived back home, we turned the horses out in the late afternoon sunshine and went straight to the pub, feeling we had earned every penny of the £200 we had been paid.

"Never, ever, again," vowed Jenny, quickly downing her second large glass of white wine.

"You can't mean it. I had a great time," Sophie said.

"Oh yes I do," Jenny replied.

And, for once, she did.

Red's finished tableau featured across a double page of the Guardian newspaper, with two Daniels appearing in opposite corners of the artwork. Jenny, Sophie and I were invited to the preview of Red's exhibition at the Impressions Gallery in Bradford. We stood with glasses of sparkling wine in front of the huge, imposing artwork and felt very proud when our horses were admired. Surrounded by cultured people in a cosy urban atmosphere, it was strange but uplifting to see Daniel and Alexander glowing in the light of an historic evening camp fire.

In 2015, Red was re-enacting the Peterloo Massacre which took place in Manchester two centuries ago. Eighteen people were killed and 700 seriously injured when cavalrymen armed with sabres rode into a gathering of protesters calling for reform.

Red is a talented, honest and good-hearted man with a genuine affection and concern for the downtrodden. His enthusiasm was infectious, but he was somewhat overoptimistic about our riding ability. So when he excitedly outlined how we would canter along and slash a water melon on a pole with a sabre, I urged him to think again.

"I'll probably slice my horse's leg off!" I protested.

Red took my point and revised his plan so we would use dummy swords for the action shots.

I took Alexander and Sprite and was joined by 18-year-old Cory Tate after Jenny refused to play any part in the venture. Cory had only recently started riding but he had a natural talent and I had let him ride Alexander, even giving the teenager a couple of informal lessons on him.

Cory – who has since graduated from racing college as the most improved jockey on his course, and is now working at a race yard in North Yorkshire – jumped at the chance of taking part in the photo shoot.

Filming was at the same location. I parked up near the entrance while we unloaded the horses and walked them up the stony track, where Pat Jones, from a local livery yard, took over their care.

I then trundled the wagon steadily up the hill towards the farm. Unfortunately, the gate at the top was closed and I had to stop. I could get no grip on the stones and dropped the horsebox back on to the grass to try to turn it round. But the ground was wet and the wagon became well and truly stuck.

Red came rushing up. "Don't worry about that. A farmer will come with his tractor to get it free. We need you guys in the costume and make-up department."

We were to dress in white patterned blousons, blue Yeoman's trousers with a white stripe down the sides, braces and a blue and white jacket with a tall peaked hat. We were both getting old-fashioned mutton chops whiskers glued to our faces for the first take. Mine were grey.

It was then time to tack up the horses in the orchard.

Alexander was a little naughty, refusing to stand next to the high wall I was using as a mounting block. Cory had no trouble getting on Sprite.

We rode into the field where the filming was to take place and I was handed my dummy sword. It was the same shape and size as a sabre, but made of light wood. At first I struggled to carry the sword while riding one-handed, which I was not used to doing anyway, and at one point I nearly poked Alexander in the cheek with it.

Red had put a bright white rope on the ground for us to canter over for the shoot. On my first trial run, Alexander took a big leap over it and I found myself flying through the air with my sword raised! But he quickly twigged what he was meant to do and kept on doing it, like a professional.

Cory and I had to canter the horses down the field and then slash and thrust with the dummy swords at imaginary peasants. As if that wasn't challenging enough, we had to roar loudly while slashing, so Red could snap our ruthless expressions. Neither of us had done anything like this before, but Red seemed pleased with our efforts.

After several similar runs up the field, Alexander was getting bored and had begun to throw himself around and try to dash off. And both horses were becoming unsettled by a group of donkeys braying loudly in the next field. So we were delighted when Red announced it was time for a break.

We joined the film crew at a huge oblong table, groaning under the weight of lunch, in the farmhouse kitchen.

I began the afternoon's filming by standing and holding a real sabre in different positions for Red to get some still shots. For half an hour I raised and lowered the sword. "Two, three, gotcha!" repeated Red, snapping away.

The sabre was heavier than I had imagined and after a while my arm was beginning to droop. A make-up girl was brought in to keep my elbow still and hold on to my side, while another had the task of balancing the point of the sabre on her finger to help keep the sword up.

Cory and I swapped mounts for the final session, which began with some static filming of the two horses together, while we posed with our swords. Then we spent forty minutes repeatedly running down the field, holding our swords aloft. Alexander was in front and going well for Cory, while Sprite scampered enthusiastically after them.

After seven long hours, the filming was done. Red was delighted and gathered everyone together to give a big round of applause to the horsemen. We touched our helmets in acknowledgment.

Finally, it was pay time. Red was writing cheques in the farmhouse, but he had an envelope full of banknotes for me. We had agreed a fee of £220, but Red counted out £250 in £50 notes.

"You've gone the extra mile," he said.

When I handed Cory his payment for the day, his face lit up. He had never seen a £50 note before.

Photo stars at the Peterloo re-enactment

Chapter Nineteen

Saddle And Silks

On Sunday, April 2, we visited Ian and Karen to collect my race saddle and silks. I was now counting down the days to the off. There were 27 of them left.

Ian had borrowed the eye-catching purple and yellow silks from one of the couple's racehorse owners. He had also fished out the special black plastic race training saddle I was to use on the big day. It looked ridiculously small and was so light I could hold it with two fingers.

"Come on," Ian said. "Put your colours on and we'll get a photo of you."

I posed for the camera with the hat silk perched at a crazy angle on my head, the tiny saddle over my arm and Ian peering over my shoulder with his thumbs up. It all looked very silly, but the fact that I now had the saddle and silks told me how serious my racing journey had become.

It was a lovely, sunny spring day and the four of us sat around a wooden table outside Alexander's old stable at the stud farm. We gazed out across the estuary, glittering in the sunlight, and tucked into scones, jam and clotted cream.

Ian tipped back his cap and asked: "How's the training going?"

"Everything seems fine so far," I replied. "We're both getting fitter."

I narrowed my eyes. "I don't know how I'll manage with this saddle, though. It looks like a postage stamp."

Karen laughed: "It will seem strange at first. Start using it straight away. Put your stirrups up. By the time you get to the race it will seem normal."

"I'll take your word for it."

"Are you going to plait Herman for the race?" asked Ian.

My horse will always be 'Herman' to him.

"No, I don't think so," said Jenny. "We'll have enough to think about. Anyway, Kauto Star was never plaited, and look what he achieved."

Ian grinned. "He ain't no Kauto Star!"

"Ah! But he's my Kauto Star!" I laughed, joining in the fun.

But then I became serious again. "Ian, you two will definitely come to the race, won't you? I want you to lead him up for me."

"Don't worry. We'll be there. And I will lead him up. I'll even pat him and talk to him in the parade ring. But that will be that!"

"You inspired me to race Alexander," I replied. "It will be a dream come true."

Ian put down his coffee mug and reached for another scone, before responding with mock gravity: "This is no dream for me."

We munched in silence, enjoying the view and each other's company. The stud farm was one of our favourite places to be. Paying to keep our three horses meant we could not afford holidays, so our day trips to Grange were special.

I was in my element there and took every opportunity to walk up the fields to see the young thoroughbreds who would be going racing. They were all beautiful but I had a soft spot for Winnie the Witch, a chestnut filly, and a liver chestnut mare called Pandora. They were both gorgeous looking animals and very affectionate. Pandora, in particular, would follow me round the field and nuzzle me for kisses.

"She's a tart," laughed Karen.

Jenny photographed me staring across the estuary from inside the big stone-built stable Alexander once occupied.

"You'll be getting one of those blue commemorative plaques for it - 'Alexander slept here!'" she joked.

As we looked out over the shimmering splendour of the estuary, the siren sounded a warning that the tide was about to turn.

"It looks beautiful but it's treacherous," said Karen. "The currents are fast and dangerous."

Those same waters had some years ago claimed the lives of a group of cockle pickers. Stranded in the dark, they stood no chance against the racing tides, said to easily outpace a galloping horse. The only way to cross the bay is with a specialist guide. Occasionally, he could be seen out in the far distance leading people across the sands, strung out like tiny black ants, and accompanied by two vehicles, small as Dinky toys in the vast waste of sea and sky.

The dangers of the estuary meant that the view from the stud farm was uncluttered by sailing boats, windsurfers and bathers. It is a bleak and natural landscape, its swirling emptiness in stark contrast to the colourful bustle of Grange-over-Sands, with its eclectic shops, cafes and flower-filled parks.

I was awed by how swiftly the waters swept in from different directions, swallowing up the last ridges of putty-coloured sand until nothing remained but a clear sweep of grey-blue water.

Jenny and I climbed up the large stack of haylage bales on the yard to see more of the spectacular view. The black plastic sheeting encasing the bales was hot and shiny in the strong afternoon sun. High overhead was the blue sky, broken by skeins of sailing cloud. To our left was the ever-changing mystery of the estuary, while to our right glowed the green fields, bright with buttercups, where the thoroughbreds grazed.

We love visiting Ian and Karen but our annual pilgrimages to see Daniel in North Wales are equally precious.

But on our visit in 2014 I found that some things never change: like his enthusiasm for chucking me off!

Daniel looked big and muscular and his black coat gleamed with health. His mane was smartly hogged and his thick, bushy tail beautifully brushed. For the first time since he had moved to his new home, I got the chance to ride him, and I was very excited by the prospect. The ladies tacked him up and stood with him outside his barn while I got on.

"Be good for your Dad," said Katie.

Daniel stood quietly as I slipped into the saddle. I grinned with delight, the moment bringing back so many fond memories.

He needed little encouragement to set off into the forest at a brisk walk.

"You show me where to go," I said, patting him, and he seemed keen to act as my guide, taking me round his wonderful mountain kingdom. We snaked our way along the woodland paths and I was surprised at his bouncy keenness.

After a few minutes, Katie said: "Do you want a trot?"

Daniel was reluctant at first but then he burst into a powerful trot through the trees, before breaking into a steady uphill canter. It was great fun.

Katie said: "There are some little logs just up ahead that we usually hop over. Do you want a go?"

"Why not?" I replied.

Jenny, struggling to keep up through the thick conifer

forest, was to say afterwards that she felt a sudden chill of foreboding.

The first log was very small and Daniel was obviously used to jumping it. Why should there be any problem? But this was me and Daniel, and nothing was ever straightforward when it came to jumping. As we trotted up to the little log, he suddenly put on the brakes and stopped.

"Daniel!" said Katie, shocked by the unexpected refusal.

Embarrassed, I turned him round and kicked him hard into the obstacle. He took off with one of his trademark jump jet leaps, and before I knew it I was sitting on the forest floor, still holding on to the reins. But Daniel determinedly tugged them from my grasp and set off at a fast canter, clattering through the undergrowth and climbing steeply upwards, deep into the forest.

I leaped up and set off in pursuit. Katie also gave chase.

Jenny was horrified by the old familiar sight of Daniel disappearing riderless into the distance.

He rapidly vanished from view but we followed the crashing sounds and then heard his hooves clattering on the lane.

"He's heading for his field," panted Katie.

I was terrified about what might happen, but it was an isolated rural area with very little traffic, and Daniel clearly knew where he was going. I dragged myself breathlessly up the last stretch of hill, fifty yards behind Katie, who suddenly called out: "It's all right. He's here."

She had caught him grazing at the gate to his field and led him back for us to be reunited.

"That's the last time I'll ever jump him," I said sheepishly.

"It's the last time you'll ever ride him," said Jenny.

Good old Dan. You can always rely on him for entertainment. I reckon he wanted to make sure I didn't take him back with me, away from his wonderful new life. He always was a clever bugger!

Saddle and silks!

Chapter Twenty

Roll Out The Wagon

With race day getting ever nearer, I was starting to worry about everything.

One of my main concerns was whether our elderly horse wagon would get Alexander to the racecourse. We had acquired it soon after coming to Farfield, replacing the Land Rover Defender which had towed our horses to events in a trailer.

The Land Rover had reached the end of the road after years of mechanical problems. Faced with yet another four-figure bill, we had to get rid of it and the trailer.

We bought the wagon, using Jenny's old pension fund, from a friend on the yard. It was a great, gleaming silver-grey beast of a thing with a maroon stripe, a 7.5 tonne Leyland Daf with space for up to three horses. It had solid and safe metal partitions, rubber-lined walls, and a new floor and ramp. There were CCTV cameras, allowing us to check on the safety of our horses as we travelled.

I had never driven such a large vehicle before but I soon learned how to keep the speed up to ensure there was enough power for uphill climbs, use the brakes and gears to slow down at junctions and roundabouts, and allow for the width and length of the vehicle when making turns.

The wagon had served us well, almost always starting at the first time of asking and trundling us safely to events. But we had a terrible drama one freezing cold day in February 2015 after taking Alexander to his first showjumping competition of the year, at the Yorkshire Riding Centre, near Harrogate.

I was excited to be competing again, and Alexander had a glint in his eye and a spring in his step. He was keen to get on with it and halfway through our first round, he put in a couple of bucks.

"Come on, don't be daft!" I chided, thinking back to when he launched me in the ring at Osbaldeston.

The winding course was not ideal for him, as it snaked around a relatively small arena. For a big, long-striding horse, there wasn't much room for manoeuvre. The turns were tight and we had to stop and start, slowing down for the corners and then pushing on into the jumps. It was a different style from our usual rhythmic, steady approach to showjumping. But Alexander answered my every call, slowing and quickening, twisting and turning, until we had jumped four clear rounds, finishing fourth in the 60cms class and fifth in the 70cms.

Afterwards, Alexander munched contentedly on his haynet, while Jenny and I celebrated with double cheeseburgers. Jenny perched on the wagon ramp, basking in the unexpected warmth of the sparkling sunshine, while I enjoyed the novelty of sitting in comfort to eat my lunch in the living quarters.

It had been eight months since Alexander last competed and he had just won two rosettes at a new venue. We were buzzing with the success of the day, but it was about to take a turn for the worse.

During our journey to the Yorkshire Riding Centre, I had been baffled by a brief loss of power as I accelerated the wagon away from a roundabout. It soon picked up again and drove perfectly normally the rest of the way. I put it down to my inexperience.

"I must have been in the wrong gear, or not pushing the

accelerator down properly," I said to Jenny.

The trip home went well until we were almost back at the yard. But as we left the Bolton Abbey roundabout to trundle the final few hundred yards to Farfield, the wagon again lost power. This time I knew I wasn't to blame.

"What's the matter with it?" asked Jenny in alarm.

"I don't know," I replied.

I kept pressing the pedal and the power returned.

"You don't think it's running out of diesel, do you?" Jenny said.

I glanced at the fuel gauge. We had set out with nearly half a tank. The indicator was now between a quarter full and the red zone. Ideally, we should have had more, but it did not seem to be at a dangerously low level.

"I don't think so. Let's just get it back and parked up."

We breathed a sigh of relief as I turned the wagon off the road and slowly started to ascend the winding drive to the yard. But halfway up the incline, and with the first stables almost within touching distance, the power went again. This time the engine cut out. I grabbed the handle for the air brakes and pulled it on. I turned the key in the ignition. The wagon had always started instantly. This time it didn't. The engine was turning over but it would not fire up. I tried again, and then a third time. Still nothing.

The wagon had stopped just above the entrance gate to the yard. The drive was narrow. Two cars could pass each other with care, if one of them trespassed on to the grass verge. But our huge vehicle was completely in the way. It was a busy Sunday afternoon and nothing could get in or out.

"I don't believe this. What are we going to do?" asked Jenny.

"I have no idea," I replied, vainly turning the key again.

Jenny unloaded Alexander and led him to his stable. Yard staff set aside their duties and came down to help, but they were equally perplexed. Then, horse owner Alex Raistrick appeared. I had clicked with Alex straight away when we came to Farfield. Like me, he had taken up riding late and owned a chestnut horse. He was willing to work hard to improve his riding and he was witty, practical and knowledgeable. I was delighted to see him. I felt he would know what to do.

Fearing we were out of fuel, he siphoned off some diesel from a barrel stashed on the yard and poured it into our tank. But the wagon still refused to start.

By now, the drive was beginning to resemble the M62. Vehicles belonging to clients and staff were stacked back towards the road, hatchbacks abandoned next to 4x4s.

"Let's try to move it out of the way," said Alex. "Drop it back on the brakes. I'll stand behind and guide you through the gate."

If we could clear a path for everybody else, we could think about the mechanical problem later. I took the handbrake off and inched back down the hill until we were between the gateposts, then I let go of the brakes. But I had little impetus and as the drive levelled off, the wagon ground to a halt. We had got through the gate but there was still not enough room for another vehicle to get past.

"For God's sake!" I exclaimed, hitting the steering wheel in frustration.

"Don't worry, we'll push it," said Alex.

All seven and a half tonnes of it!

A small army of helpers had now gathered, among them staff members. They were finding this much more fun than skipping out and filling haynets.

Everyone shoved but the great wagon just stood there gleaming in the sun and refusing to budge.

"Is the brake off?" asked Alex.

"Yes," I called back, surreptitiously checking.

The battalion heaved once more. The wagon did not move.

"Right!" said Alex. "I'll fetch my car. We'll shove it with that."

"You can't do that," I protested.

Alex's car was a smart and gleaming black Land Rover Defender.

"I can," he called, dashing off.

He reappeared behind the wheel and nosed the Land Rover into position. The shiny surfaces of the front of Alex's vehicle and our wagon were padded for protection with someone's brand new white sheepskin girth guard and a chunky cushion from the wagon's living quarters.

"I was never that keen on the beige upholstery," said Jenny, trying to make light of the situation, but we both wished the ground would swallow us up.

Alex revved his engine. There was an alarming cracking sound from the wagon's front bumper and a burning smell from the Land Rover's clutch.

"Stop! Stop! You'll ruin your lovely car," shouted Jenny, by now almost in tears.

It was time to call in the cavalry, in the shape of Jane and the yard's powerful Manitou machine. This impressive contraption was used for all sorts of pulling, pushing and lifting jobs. Great, thick chains were attached to the front for hoisting heavy pieces of machinery from place to place. Now it faced its biggest challenge, to drag our wagon up the drive.

Jane immediately took charge.

"Go and help the girls to skip out," she told Jenny. "I'll take care of this."

With Alex's help, Jane attached the great chains from the Manitou around the wagon's bumper and carefully put her machine into reverse. I watched from the cab, clinging to the steering wheel in resigned silence, expecting nothing to go right. There was a great clunk and for a couple of seconds I felt the wagon inch forward. Then there was a big judder and the chain snapped free.

I wrenched on the brake as Alex scurried to reattach the chain. Jane sat calm and impassive in the Manitou.

I felt it was a hopeless cause and we would be marooned on the drive forever. But Jane was determined and after a couple more heavy clunks I was astonished to see the Manitou backing slowly up the drive, with me and the wagon sliding after it. I say sliding because the back brakes had seized.

Although I clung on to the steering wheel, we were rudderless, like a huge stricken ship being dragged along by a small but powerful tugboat.

Making it look much easier than it actually was, Jane towed us up, foot by endless foot, on to the yard. I feared the chain would snap at any moment, but it didn't.

The wagon's wheels had locked as it was dragged up the drive, leaving great lines in the surface where they had cut through it. I thought our horsebox could be stuck where it was for a long time.

But I had reckoned without the expert service of local mechanic Stuart Lambert. A couple of days after the breakdown, we arrived at Farfield to find the wagon had gone. Stuart had ridden to the rescue. He had got it started and nursed it over the moors to his garage.

"She'd normally fly over those hills," he told us. "She was losing power but I kept teasing her along, and we got back by hook or by crook."

Before the end of the week Stuart had repaired the wagon.

"I think she got a gob full of air," he explained, meaning that there was a blockage in the system caused when the fuel tank got low around the undulating hairpin bends on Blubberhouses Moor.

With the race now so close I was taking the wagon out for a spin a couple of times a week. The thing about old wagons like ours is you have to keep running them. If you leave them parked up for weeks they just won't start up. And worn out little connections and leads in the engine compartment can also leave you stranded. I hoped my regular twenty-minute drives would be enough to keep our vehicle in tip-top order.

I was reassured by an emergency back up plan that Charles had put in place. "The Farfield trailer is good to go, should it be needed," he told me. If anything should go wrong with the wagon on the morning of the race, we would still be able to get Alexander there.

Jenny and Sprite at Camp Hill

Chapter Twenty-One

Our Kingdom For A Horse

In 2016, Jenny and I moved in as lodgers with Jane Barker at Farfield Farm. We were fleeing yet another financial crisis.

We had slid into serious debt and at the start of the year Jenny put her cottage on the market. By March we had a buyer for it and we were house hunting. We were swapping village life in the Yorkshire Dales for a more urban environment, where the properties were cheaper, but we didn't care. We would be out of debt. No more high interest bank loans we could never pay off and spiralling credit card debt. No more feeling sick every time we checked our horrendously overdrawn bank balances at the cash machine.

"We have sold our kingdom for a horse – or three horses," Jenny said.

We wouldn't have had it any other way. But our house buying budget was very modest. We were looking at the lower end of the market and couldn't find anything worth even viewing.

"If I see another gloomy looking terraced house with no garden and nowhere to park, I will scream," said Jenny.

And then we found what we were searching for; the pretty little cottage destined to be our first home together.

"What do you think?" asked Jenny. "It looks quite nice and it's very cheap."

I peered over her shoulder at the internet property site to

see an attractive little stone built house with pots of flowers clustered in front of it. It was new on the market and we rushed to view it. The cottage had once been part of a big house and had many original features, including wooden floors, a stone-flagged basement, beams, fireplaces and wide alcoves. There was an enclosed back garden and room to park on the quiet back street that wound its way up on to the moors. The purchase price would leave us with enough cash to pay for the home improvements we wanted to make, as well as clear all our debts. The little old lady who owned the cottage was keen to press ahead with the sale, but a few weeks down the line she told us there was a long waiting list at the sheltered housing she wanted to go to. The deal now looked like taking many months. We were in limbo and feared we could end up homeless. But we were about to land on our feet.

"Why don't you move in with me?" said Jane one day. "I've loads of room. It will give you the space you need to get sorted with your house."

On a beautiful spring morning in May, we packed up our belongings and moved out of Jenny's house. We put most of our things into storage but kept our treasures with us, including our equestrian photos, rosettes and trophies.

We had never set foot in Jane's ancient stone farmhouse before. It stands sentinel above the rows of stables, with stunning views from the back straight out across the fields and woods. The tasteful and stylish grandeur of the place, with its original tiled hall and beautiful big kitchen, was a striking contrast to the tired old cottage we had sold. After the cold, the dark, the rain and the poverty, we were walking out into the light. It was a fresh start with renewed hope. We marvelled that we would be staying in such a house, and it was two weeks before Jenny even dared to boil the kettle.

On our first day at the farmhouse, we walked out of the

back door into the sparkling sunshine. We opened the little wicket gate into Alexander's field and strolled across the spring grass to say hello to him. We passed Sprite and Dixie, grazing on the other side of a high stone wall, crossed another meadow into Bluebell Woods, and ambled beside the gently flowing River Wharfe until we reached the Devonshire Arms Brasserie. We sat outside in the warm sunshine, taking in the panoramic views across to the wooded hills, and counted our blessings.

Living at Farfield gave us the once in a lifetime privilege of being at home with our horses. We could wander down to Top Barn and say goodnight to them before retiring to bed. It was a simple but hugely fulfilling act. In the daytime, the magnificent view from our bedroom window at the back of the house meant we could see all three of our horses grazing happily in their lush meadows. On weekend mornings, we sat on the king size bed and watched them being turned out. Heads nodding, Sprite and Dixie passed by with their friends down the track. They were led through the open gate and released beneath the large tree at the entrance to their meadow. I never failed to be excited by the little procession marching purposefully along for their day out.

"Is that Dixie in front?" I said, straining my eyes to pick her out.

"Here comes Sprite. You can tell its her by the way she flicks her tail," announced Jenny, watching with pride and trepidation as her little mare bustled from the gate and energetically rolled over and over close to an outcrop of stone. Dixie calmly sauntered across to stand confidently on the top of the rock, observing her surroundings like an equine Monarch of the Glen guarding her small herd from any possible threat from lions, tigers and bears marauding down from the nearby hills.

Just above the field runs a belt of trees marking the old

railway line, known as Puddle Path, and the pasture slopes gently down to woodland carpeted with bluebells and yellow buttercups in the spring. By October, the trees have turned into flaring beacons of red, russet and gold.

Leaving the picturesque beauty of Farfield Farm on those dazzling sunny mornings to drive to work in Bradford was like moving from light into deep shade. They were as different as night and day.

But coming home was always uplifting. As we journeyed back, the grim urban buildings gave way to fields, where sheep, cattle and horses grazed. The River Wharfe tumbled energetically beside the main road as we made our way to Ilkley. We then skirted the edge of the attractive village of Addingham and swept along a country road towards Bolton Abbey, passing the familiar sight of a lone Highland cow in her pasture alongside a rambling property reached by an old stone hump-back bridge. Across to our right, beyond the tree-lined fields and the hidden folds of the river, rose steep, grassy hills, leading to the summit of Beamsley Beacon, standing guard over the land as men of old had done from a tower there. We eased round a hairpin bend, flanked by high walls, and at a swinging sign depicting a prancing black horse, turned sharp left on to the drive that winds its way to Farfield.

One Friday evening, after travelling home from Bradford, I reversed into my parking spot next to the lawn, took a deep breath and exhaled slowly and contentedly. Now I could relax. It was well after six o'clock but the stables were still bathed in sunlight. I was too tired to ride but I wanted to see our horses and I immediately strode the short distance to Top Barn.

Sprite's stable is just outside the entrance to the barn, while the other two live inside the building. As I rounded the corner I saw that Sprite's bright bay head, with its big white star, was over her door as usual, looking out to see what was happening on the main yard. I gave mints to her and Dixie and turned to Alexander's stable. I felt a deep contentment and joy as his long nose, with its crooked white blaze, reached out to gently nudge me for his mint.

"Here you are, Man," I said, using his pet name and gazing affectionately into his deep, brown eyes. I stroked his nose as he crunched the treat. We had been together for more than half his life and there was no doubt that he had changed mine.

"Have you had a good day?" I asked.

Alexander stared back at me, but his muddy legs and head told me he'd had great fun out in the field. I made his supper and watched in silence as he eagerly devoured it, shoving his black rubber dish aside with his nose as he scooped up the remaining nuts and mix he had spilled in his excitement. Then he raised his head for another mint.

Later that evening, Jenny and I strolled down to see the horses together. Stars twinkled brightly in the clear, inky black sky. The big moon shone a white light across the yard. Shadows in dark corners were chased away by the strong yellow security lights. It was nearly ten o'clock and Farfield was at peace. The livery yard clients were long gone and the metal gate at the bottom of the drive was locked for the night. The horses tucked into their haynets or slumbered in their stables. The silence was broken only by the occasional snort of a horse and the hoot of an owl somewhere in the dark belt of trees behind the outdoor school.

Saturday dawned cloudy and fresh. There was an early morning chill in the air as the staff turned out the horses. I peered out from the bedroom window across to Alexander's pasture. It was not yet eight o'clock and the field was still empty. But looking to my left I could see lines of horses being led up the stony track. In the distance, I thought I could make out Sprite and Dixie. Alexander and his chums would be the last out. But it would soon be their turn.

"I'm going outside to watch for him," I told Jenny, before dashing downstairs in my dressing gown.

I opened the back door, stepped on to the grass and stood looking over the low wall towards the gate to Alexander's field. I was just in time. As I watched, the gate was opened. Eight horses were led in by the staff. One by one the girls slipped off the head collars to release them. The horses were always eager to go out, but this morning they were especially keen. The freshness of the air and a slight breeze had made them frisky. They began cantering joyously down the field, some bucking with delight.

I could see Alexander at the back, still being held by Charles. He seemed to be behaving and when Charles let him go, he strolled nonchalantly forward, sniffing the air. Suddenly, Alexander lowered his head and arched his neck in front of his chest. For a moment his body seemed to constrict into a pent up ball of energy. Then he stretched out his neck, the energy was released and he started to run. He held his body low to the ground, defying the resistance of the air like an Olympic sprinter, and was instantly flying along at a flat out gallop. Within a few strides he had overtaken his pals, passing them as if they were running on the spot, and disappeared into the distance.

Charles, who had spotted me taking it all in from my grandstand vantage point, grinned and shouted across: "He thinks he's racing again!"

It had been spectacular and reminded me, not for the first time, of the speed and athleticism of my horse. It had proved my downfall on many occasions in our early years together. Sometimes I had been frightened but now my fear had gone and I just enjoyed riding him.

The next day would bring a new challenge - our first British

Eventing cross-country course. It was part of a one-day event, at Breckenbrough in North Yorkshire, involving dressage, and showjumping and cross-country at a height of 80cms. Over the years, Alexander and I had become a serious eventing partnership but fences at BE standard were a big step up.

I walked the course on Saturday afternoon with Emilly Thane, who was also competing at the event. It soon became apparent that while the height of the fences was restricted to 80cms, the width of them knew no bounds. We marvelled at the size of some of them, but did not feel daunted - until we came to the big table fence, two thirds of the way round the course. It was solid, deep, and must have been five feet wide.

We studied it and looked at each other in trepidation. There was a long silence and then I voiced our thoughts. "Bloody hell, that's big!"

I looked hard at the fence and came to a decision.

"The only way to ride this is to gallop at it and go for it."

But even as I uttered the words it seemed much easier to say than do.

Back at Farfield, Jenny anxiously asked what I thought about the course. She had been busily preparing for the event, cleaning the tack and smartening up Alexander. She had done a brilliant job and he looked a picture with his neatly plaited orange mane.

"It's big, as you'd expect it to be," I replied. "But there's plenty of places to gallop. He'll love it."

I turned to Alexander, who looked relaxed in his stable.

"Are you ready for tomorrow?" I said, as he nibbled contentedly at his haynet.

He glanced at me out of the corner of his eye, sighed deeply as if to say: "What do you think?" and carried on eating.

I patted his long neck. "You'll be ready."

It was bright and sunny on Sunday. Not ideal for Alexander

because of his allergy, but I wasn't worried about it affecting his performance. Certainly not in the cross-country phase. Dressage was our weak link. Alexander was bred to run and jump, so the bending and shaping disciplines of dressage did not come easily to him, or me! His task was not helped by his allergy, which caused him to throw his head around – not what the judges were looking for.

Sure enough, we were trailing after the dressage and when we had four faults in the showjumping we were well out of contention for a place. All that remained was to enjoy ourselves in the cross-country and we intended to do just that.

Alexander had got himself quite wound up and his neck was damp with the sweat of nervous excitement as we waited to set off. The crackle of the on-course commentary was a noisy reminder of his racing days, and having to stand in an enclosed starting box for the first time only added to his tension.

I tried to soothe him by stroking his neck and whispering: "You're all right," but still he was on edge.

The starter counted us down: "Three, two, one - go! Good luck."

We emerged sideways from the starting box, with Alexander tossing his head and prancing. For a few frantic seconds, I thought our round was over before it had begun. But I managed to kick him forward and suddenly we were off.

Now Alexander channelled all his nervous energy into the job he loved to do. He galloped towards the first fence and, without breaking stride, soared over it. His pace didn't slacken as we jumped the next, nor as we climbed a hill and turned to leap the chunky third obstacle. We slowed as we went through a thin copse of trees and jumped a tricky little fence after it. Then I gave him a squeeze with my lower leg and we were off again, speeding across the field on a long run to the next set of jumps.

As we raced along, the commentator announced: "This beautiful ex-racehorse has really set sail!"

Galloping Alexander is a thrill. He is so smooth and sure-footed you seem to be floating ethereally above the ground. But at the same time you feel like you are being whisked through the air by a great wind. It is a unique experience. It must have looked good to the spectators, but I was in the best seat in the house. This was exactly why I had wanted Alexander, to tow me round a challenging cross-country course, leaping everything in our path.

"This is brilliant, Man," I shouted, as we bowled along.

Now we were approaching The Big Table, which had looked so enormously wide from the ground. I held my nerve and kicked Alexander into it. I didn't need to. There was no holding him back. He stormed in, stood off, and soared over it as if it wasn't there. I felt as if I was flying and we seemed to hang in the air for several seconds as his great leap cleaved through it.

Then we were galloping across the grass again.

"Good lad, that was fab!" I called, and his ears twitched in response.

The end of the course was now in sight. We cantered exuberantly through the water complex and set up for the final log. And then we were racing over the finish line. Alexander seemed ready to go round again and we were nearly back at the start before I managed to pull him up. I dismounted, and patted his neck with exuberant delight. Alexander was sweating and puffing gently from his exertions. His nostrils were flared but there was a look in his eyes of pure satisfaction.

I put my arms round his neck and hugged him. "Thanks lad. That was amazing."

Jenny came dashing up. "Well done. Are you all right?"

"Never better. What a thrill."

"I'm so proud of you both," she said. "You have come so far."

Indeed we had. Just a few weeks earlier, we had won the 70cms class in the first Camp Hill Mini Hunter Trial of the series. Now we were jumping BE courses.

Soon afterwards, Alexander and I tackled an 80cms one-day event at Northallerton Equestrian Centre. This time we were placed, despite being last after the dressage. Another thrilling cross-country round hauled us up the order to finish eighth.

It seemed no coincidence that our willingness to take on bigger courses, and have a measure of success, had followed our move to Farfield. Alexander had never been happier or healthier, while my confidence had grown as I was able to devote more time to riding him. Farfield suited me down to the ground and that was now being reflected in our preparations for the race.

Jumping new heights at Camp Hill (Chris Lux Event Photography)

Chapter Twenty-Two

Another Racer

Our seven-month stay at Jane's farmhouse passed all too quickly. By September 2016, we had possession of our little cottage. To keep within our budget, we did much of the renovation work ourselves; painting the walls and ceilings, scrubbing and varnishing the floors, and ripping out unwanted cupboards and drawers, including the entire kitchen. We lived at Farfield while we did the work but by the end of November, our home was ready to move into.

We gathered up the latest photos of Alexander in cross-country action, which we had displayed on the sitting room window sill at Farfield, and made a new 'Shelves of Greatness' at our cottage. Jenny created The Shelves at our old house as a special tribute to my competing success with Alexander. The little shrine, with its colourful rosettes and photos of us in action, next to a picture of Alexander leaping a fence in his racing days, marks our modest achievements.

I frequently gaze at The Shelves with wonder and pride, and sometimes have to pinch myself to believe it is me riding such a terrific athlete. For me, they tell a story. A personal one of success against the odds, and of happy times.

One new addition to The Shelves is particularly special to me.

Alexander and I rounded off our 2016 outdoor season by

competing for the first time in the Hunter Trials at Craven Country Ride. The event is always challenging. The steep, hilly terrain is a test of stamina and David Coates builds solid and chunky fences.

Years ago, I had steered a reluctant Daniel round the course – every time I stopped kicking he went back to a walk! But I had never been a real contender. On my ex-racehorse things could be different.

When I walked the course, the evening before the event, it filled me with excitement. But I took a deep breath when I came to the huge, wide brush fence David had constructed at the exit to the water complex.

"Alexander will think he's steeplechasing again when he sees that," I said.

David grinned back at me.

"What are you worried about, Steve? He is a steeplechaser!"

When I first took Alexander to Craven Country Ride, and had two crashing falls in one day, David's tactful and concerned response was: "Rome wasn't built in a day, Steve."

Now he thought I was up to the challenge.

David was proved right. When Alexander cantered through the water, he needed only three long strides to reach the big brush fence. He stood off it and flew over, giving it plenty of daylight. I was delighted to finish tenth out of forty in our class. I was even prouder to receive a special Retraining of Racehorses rosette for Alexander being the highest placed of the six ex-racers competing. The green and white ribbon, embossed with pictures of a racehorse before and after retraining, is a fantastic addition to The Shelves, along with a photo of Alexander and I taking a mighty leap during our round.

One of my favourite purchases for the cottage is a big print of the We Three Kings painting of jumps racing legends Arkle, Red Rum and Desert Orchid. I picked it up cheaply at a local antiques centre and the trio of Kings look grandly down on me as I work at my desk in a corner of the stone-flagged basement.

Spending my days working from home led to the fulfillment of another long-held wish. By the New Year of 2017, another ex-racer had come into our lives, although this one was much smaller than Alexander and had enjoyed considerable success on the track.

We had not owned a dog since the death of our beloved lurcher Denny, fondly known by family and friends as Mrs Dog.

Jenny had owned Mrs Dog since she was a puppy, swapping her for a single bed. She was a mixture of greyhound, collie and stag hound, and everything about her was long. She had a gentle, sweet nature, a huge appetite for titbits, and liked nothing more than to curl up in my comfortable chair in front of the log burning stove. Her chin resting comfortably on the chair arm, she gazed across at us with big, brown eyes. I enjoyed wonderful holidays with Mrs Dog in Scotland, where she sailed by ferry boat to the Isle of Mull and climbed up mountains, and in Norfolk, where she romped for miles on the sandy beaches.

Approaching her fourteenth birthday, she had slowed down a bit but she still loved her walks on the village green, wading across the river when it was low or skipping over the stepping stones.

On Easter Monday, 2011, we were returning from our morning river walk when Mrs Dog collapsed from some sort of catastrophic seizure. I carried her home in my arms and laid her on her favourite doggy cushion in the kitchen. We summoned the vet but there was nothing that could be done and she was put to sleep. She slipped away quickly and peacefully on her cushion, with her family around her. We were heartbroken. She was terribly missed and the flowered urn containing her ashes remained on the shelf in the tack room at home, while her lead, collar and coat hung untouched behind the pantry door. Her urn came with us to Farfield and it is still there, on the window sill in the back bedroom, where she can look out across the fields that she would have had so much fun in.

For a long time we were unable to think about getting another dog, but now we were making a new beginning, and the time felt right.

"I really want another hound, and I want it to be a rescue dog," said Jenny. "There are so many needing homes."

We contacted the Greyhound Trust, a wonderful charity that has rehomed more than 60,000 racing greyhounds over the years. Kath Armitage, from the Trust, came to see us, to assess the sort of dog that would suit us and our lifestyle, and to ensure that we, and our home, were suitable. We passed the test.

The next step was to visit the kennels, near Pontefract, where some of the dogs were being kept as they waited for new homes. We were excited and nervous as we drove down the motorway. Choosing the doggy person to complete our family would be a big decision.

We were shown three recently retired greyhounds. They were all bitches, which tend to be smaller and less lively than the males. The kennel staff took them into a special enclosed run, where they were exercised, so we could get to know them. We bent down and stroked them and took each of them for a walk. They were all beautiful and deserving of good homes. But one of them appeared to have chosen us. Like Innes and Dixie before her, she seemed to be saying: "Take me."

Glenvale Betty, to use her racing name, was less sure of herself than the other two. When I walked her down the long pen she trotted along beside me, gazing up at me with her deep brown eyes, like bright marbles. Even when the other two dogs were let off their leads for a run, Betty stayed by my side and did not try to join them.

"She's really sucking up to you," smiled one of the staff.

Betty was black with a white bib, white feet and a white tip to her tail. She was quiet and her soft eyes were unblinking when she looked at us.

We spent a few minutes longer around the three dogs before they were taken back to the kennels.

"We'll leave you to have a think and a chat," said the kennels boss.

Jenny and I looked at each other.

"What do you think? They're all lovely," said Jenny.

"They are," I replied. "But Betty is particularly sweet. I think she would fit in well. And she obviously wants to come with us."

"I agree. But we can't call her Betty, it sounds like Some Mothers Do 'Ave 'Em!"

We discussed names and settled on Lily.

Three days after Christmas, we went back to the kennels, paid a donation to the charity and put Lily in the back of the car. She was spayed and had been given all her injections a couple of weeks earlier. That morning she had been wormed and bathed. She came with a collar, lead and muzzle, as well as a booklet and leaflets with advice about caring for a greyhound, and we bought a warm coat for her and a fleecy bedtime vest from the charity.

Lily travelled quietly, lying down for the entire journey. When we arrived at the cottage, she ventured bravely through the front door and nervously began to explore. We had been told that greyhounds can take time to adapt. Racers have known only the track and the kennels, so living in a house would be a wholly new experience. We were advised to be patient and to encourage good behaviour, rather than punish bad. I had learned to be tolerant with Alexander after he arrived fresh off the track and like him, Lily had found herself on the scrapheap at an early age. She was only two years old. She had raced thirty times in just six months, winning on six occasions and coming second six times. But her form had tailed off.

"She did a lot better than Alexander," Jenny remarked.

We bought a tartan dog basket and put it in the basement, along with Lily's bowls for food and water on a special stand. The basement, leading to the enclosed garden, would be her security, her place of safety. At first she was reluctant to leave it, spending the day curled up in her basket in front of the radiator. When it came to walk time, she looked nervously at the steep, winding steps up to the kitchen. She would never have seen steps before and these were not easy. Lily felt unable to tackle them. For the first week, I had to carry her up and down them. It was good exercise for me as she weighed twenty six kilos and was muscular. Negotiating the awkward stairs with a heavy dog dangling from my arms was a challenge. Then she started to put her front legs on the lower steps and assess the ascent. One day she took the plunge and came bounding up to the kitchen, her legs skittering on its wooden floor, but she still spent most of the time in the basement.

"I wish she'd come and join us in the evenings," said Jenny, but it couldn't be rushed.

Gradually, Lily began to come upstairs more and one evening she flopped down on the rug in front of us. It wasn't long before we had to buy a big doggy cushion for her to sleep on in the living room. It was weeks before she ventured upstairs to the bedrooms, but once she did, she made the landing outside our room her new sleeping place, on the 'Lilypad' we then had to buy her.

Lily was settling in well at home but it took much longer for her to get used to the outside world. She was nervous around strangers, particularly men, and terrified of other dogs. The smaller the dog, the more frightened she was, pulling frantically away from them on the end of her lead, however friendly they were trying to be.

One dreadful night, soon after she arrived, Lily broke away from me in the park near to our cottage and ran home in the dark. I chased after her in horror, frantically shouting her name in a desperate bid to stop her before she reached the main road. A black dog running over that road at night stood little chance. Appalling memories of my nightmare pursuit of Alexander when he broke loose on the road came back to me, and I could only watch, sickened and helpless, as Lily sped on to the busy carriageway. How she survived, I don't know. There must have been a gap in the traffic, and she is fleet of foot. She made it. I caught up with her in front of our cottage, still shouting her name. She was terrified. She backed into the wall, barking and growling at me. I yelled to Jenny and she came out and coaxed Lily indoors. It was a nasty experience that left me badly shaken. Jenny bought a stronger lead for Lily and I now wrap my hand securely through the leather handle and round the chain to ensure she never escapes again.

Lily was more confident at the stables and perfectly relaxed around the horses. Sprite was wary of her and Dixie indifferent. Alexander offered her friendship, stretching his long neck to touch noses with her.

Lily learned to climb the steps into the living area of the horse wagon and was soon joining us on trips out to events, lying on the comfy bench seat and looking out of the window. Alexander notched up three indoor showjumping wins with Lily part of the team. But the new outdoor season was almost upon us and this one would begin on the racetrack.

Chapter Twenty-Three

Galloping On!

After our successful spin round the Crow Wood gallops with Emilly and Joe, I decided to keep working Alexander with other horses when I could. I felt the more he ran with them, the better able he would be to deal with a hectic race situation.

I had no shortage of willing helpers. Sue Dinsdale was the first to assist during her regular Tuesday hack out on Alexander. Sue is hugely experienced with racehorses. She has ridden them for many years and led them up at the races for local trainer, Pat Fitton. Alexander doesn't faze Sue, even in his livelier moods. She is very fond of him and he cares for and respects her in return.

With a little over three weeks to the race, I saddled Dixie to join Sue on her ride out.

"What can I do to help?" Sue asked.

"It's a hill work training day. Are you all right with some trotting and cantering uphill?"

"Of course, as long as we're in control!"

"Don't worry, Alexander's actually fairly laid back about his training."

It was Dixie who looked more like a racehorse, as she cantered enthusiastically at the front.

Then I had an idea.

"I want to see if Alexander will come past another horse.

We haven't tried that yet. If I hold Dixie in a slow canter, would you ask Alexander to overtake?"

But Dixie, whose mother was a racehorse, became frustrated as I kept her at a steady pace, and pulled to go faster. And when Alexander ranged up alongside, Dixie immediately grabbed the bit, quickened and took him on. We raced to the gate at the top of the hill, where we pulled up safely.

I laughed. "Well, that was an eye opener. Dixie has certainly got a competitive head on her. How was Alexander?"

"More than happy to go past," replied Sue. "And when Dixie went faster, he was eager to respond."

Sophie, on Sprite, was next to join in with the race training. The pair loved it as we did fast canter work in the fields. Alexander immediately surged past Sprite when I asked him to. It seemed he was feeling competitive. Jenny watched proudly as her little mare broke into a fast gallop, skipping nimbly over the grass like a racing pony. She was surprised and impressed by Sprite's slick and enthusiastic turn of speed.

Then it was the turn of Peter Mawson, who was part-loaning Dixie, to come to the party. We had a couple of excellent training sessions, with Dixie thundering along hard on Alexander's heels.

Jane had seen us going flat out as she and her staff were bringing in the horses from an adjoining field. She told Jenny: "Alexander went galloping past Dixie, who did a half-rear and went flying after him. The gentlemen looked very secure and they both had red faces and broad grins when they walked back down the track!"

I was using my racing saddle every time I rode Alexander. It had felt tiny at first, almost as if I was riding bareback, but I had quickly got used to it. I was sometimes a bit wobbly when we were trotting, but I felt secure when we went faster and I had cantered downhill without a problem. Riding with shorter stirrups was helping.

Emilly had been keen to see the flimsy saddle at close quarters. Jenny balanced it on the door of the feeding area in Top Barn while the pair contemplated it.

"Rather him than me," mused Emilly.

"He's going to die using that," replied Jenny. "I have spent the last seven years trying to make him as secure as possible on that horse, and keep it as chilled as I could. Now he's ramping the horse up to full fitness and planning to race on that tiny thing. God help us!"

Jenny had put Alexander's orange racing reins back on his bridle. I had stuffed them in a drawer years ago after telling myself he was no longer a racehorse, following another of my high speed crashing falls. With the reins; an Irish martingale, worn by most racehorses; and an eye-catching yellow-trimmed saddle cloth we had bought for the race, he was really looking the part.

I could see that Alexander was leaner and more muscular, and I was not alone in noticing. When I led him past a farrier shoeing another horse at the yard, he took one look at Alexander and exclaimed: "Fuck me! It looks like Aldaniti," referring to the famous Grand National winner.

Jane instantly quipped: "Not when it is wearing its big mesh fly hat, it doesn't!"

Our equine physiotherapist, Angela Brock, confirmed Alexander's gleaming good health when she gave him a special pre-race sporting massage. As she pummelled him, karate-style, she said: "He's in super condition. He has got more muscle, and it is both firm and elastic, which is ideal. And I haven't seen better hamstrings in a long time!"

Angela's written assessment gave Alexander all round good marks for his back, legs, head, neck and tail. She concluded: "Can't find anything to report! Good luck."

Friends on Facebook might have wondered when I later publicly thanked Angela for 'The Chinese massage!' and she replied: "You're very welcome. But it was Swedish!"

I was beginning to believe I could take Alexander back into a highly charged racing environment and survive it. With a fortnight to go, I was also confident he was close to race fitness. It was hard to know for sure because I had never ridden a race fit horse, but he felt and looked fantastic. And he continued to showing the same self-control and discipline in training that he had always done when we competed.

Friends were still offering advice, although my panel of experts had slightly different opinions about my final preparations. Keith Rosier suggested a good gallop now and a short, fast piece of work the day before the race, a view echoed by David Coates. Wendy Wild advised two gallops in the final week, while Michael McNeela thought I should keep increasing the fast work. It was all helpful, if a tad confusing. And the final decision on what to do in the last few days had to be mine.

All my advisers were united about one thing – not to overdo the training. The phrase kept cropping up: "Don't run your race before the race." I had to deliver Alexander at peak fitness on the day. That meant taking my foot off the accelerator at the right time. For now, we had to keep pushing.

On Easter Monday, we did a short piece of uphill canter work, with a good gallop thrown in. Two days later, we did steep hill work in trot, or a slow, bouncy canter, which had him blowing and sweating, and on Thursday we had four fairly fast canters up the long hillside known as Lob Wood Pasture. Alexander found it easy and was actually quite lazy to begin with, but became more enthusiastic with each run.

My mind was turning to race tactics. I still did not know how many runners were in our race, or what the strength of the opposition was, so I had not decided whether to go from the front or stalk from behind. What I did know was that I would be trying to win.

David Coates' daughter, Sally, a point-to-point rider who had ridden the Skipton course many times, told me to give Alexander a breather at the top of the hill and then squeeze him on down the other side to the finish.

Sally added: "If you are not near the front at the top of the hill, you won't win."

The nearer the race drew, the more I felt the pressure to perform. Getting the saddle and the silks had hyped it up. I had also written an article for the local Craven Herald newspaper about us racing.

I told Emilly: "I only did it to market the book. But I'm putting myself up there. I hope I'm not setting us up to fail."

It may have been misconceived, but I suddenly felt there was an expectation for me to do well on my ex-racehorse.

Now I put plans in place to capture every moment of what I hoped would be an unforgettable day, for all the right reasons. Justin McChesney, who had recently arrived at Farfield with his chestnut horse Henry the Great, offered to lend me his new £300 head cam to wear during the race. It would record every stride from my jockey's eye. I prayed it would not show the ground at close quarters!

Mike Simmonds, a photographer pal from the Telegraph & Argus, agreed to come along and make a video of our day. It would start with our preparations at the yard and take in the race and its aftermath. Mike is a talented video journalist and I knew the end product would provide me with special memories for the rest of my life. If all went well, it would be a joy to watch Alexander's Big Day Out from the comfort of the cosy living room at our new home.

Chapter Twenty-Four

The Final Countdown

Saturday, April 22, 2017

The countdown to the race was now well and truly on. In just seven days my dream would be a reality. Alexander would once again be a racehorse. My nerves were really starting to jangle.

I had continued to use Alexander's racing name, Adelphi Warrior, when we competed. It was said to be bad luck to change it, but anyway I thought it was a good name. Soon it would be heard on the racecourse again.

The organisers had told us we would not be able to walk the course until a set time on the morning of the race. I was disappointed. Before riding in a race you ought to walk the course as many times as you feel is necessary, to check the ground for any nasty holes or divets to avoid and to work out where you want to be during the race and what lines you want to take. I do the same before showjumping or going round a cross-country course. I had wanted to walk round the racetrack at least twice, if not three times, so I could make a clear plan about where I wanted us to be positioned.

I decided to have an early look at the course anyway. It is on private farmland, so I knew I wouldn't be able to get up close but I thought the mere sight of it, even from a distance, might inspire and calm me.

I parked up as near as I could and gazed across towards the track. The great steeplechase fences were in place. Even from several hundred yards away, they looked huge and I felt relieved that I would not be jumping them.

I looked towards the distant hill and began to mentally ride round the course.

"That's where we'll start. We'll run down the hill, past the winning post, and round the big, sweeping bend. Then we head away and up the steep hill on the other side, round the top of it, and back down again to the finish."

It sounded simple put like that.

It would probably take us about four minutes to complete the course. It didn't seem very long, for all the effort we had put into our training.

I stared silently towards the track, trying to picture Alexander and I on it, but the image was not yet coming through.

Sunday, April 23

"I didn't expect to be dressing you!" Ian exclaimed, as he shoved my lower left leg inside the tight-fitting, knee-length black riding boot.

I was in the kitchen at Ian and Karen's house at Grange-over-Sands. He had called me a few days earlier.

"We've got the rest of your jockey gear. Come and collect it and we'll do a photo fashion shoot. Don't forget your silks and hat, but don't bring the ginger donkey!"

When we got to the stud farm I was ushered indoors with a big blue sports bag. It contained white racing breeches; a black lycra undershirt; skull cap; felt whip; goggles; a racing body protector; and the long black boots – everything a jockey would need. Indeed, it belonged to a former jockey who was now a trainer.

The kit had been washed and was spotless. Everything fitted well apart from the boots. My calves had got thicker with the training and we strained and shoved in a huge effort to get the zips up.

"Bend your leg," Ian instructed, kneeling beside me and shovelling my leg into the boot with one hand while yanking the zip with the other. After several minutes we managed to get the zip up most of the way, but the boot was pinching me.

"I don't know where to look," said Karen, arriving in the kitchen as I wrestled with the body protector's elastic strapping, which had to be pulled between my legs and fastened at the front.

At last I was ready and I marched out on to the yard, twirling the whip between two fingers.

"You look like a proper jockey," Ian declared.

After posing for photos, I put everything carefully back in the bag and we sat on the stableyard, drinking coffee and tucking in to our favourite scones.

Ian had some final words of advice.

"Make sure of two things on Saturday. Don't fall off, and don't finish last!"

"Just enjoy it," Karen added.

The last few days flew by in a whirl of worry and fear. Looking back, I can remember little about them.

I ticked off each day that Alexander came safely in from the field. I was terrified he would get himself kicked. Any injury now would end my racing dream.

Even Charles was getting anxious.

"I want to wrap Alexander in cotton wool until race day," he said one evening.

Charles had taken my race saddlecloth to a friend and had farfieldlivery.com embroidered on the side of it. After all the support I'd had from Jane and Charles, it seemed right to carry the yard name into battle.

As planned, I eased back on our training, concentrating in the last week on gentle walks, a few steady canters and some uphill trotting.

On Friday – the day before the race - we did our last piece of fast work. I chose a long, steep field and identified a diagonal run across the meadow where it sloped more gently. We did one controlled canter and followed it with two quick gallops, which Alexander did easily.

We pranced back to the yard. Alexander seemed in very good heart and I felt he was fit and ready. Our work was now complete. There was no more to be done. Except wait. And worry.

I now knew who we would be racing against. There were to be two charity races, with seven runners in each. We were in the first and one of our rivals was John Chadwick, who had set us off at Coniston Hunter Trials two years ago. John is a leading light in the local hunt, as brave as they come and very competitive. He was riding a horse called Willis. A sneaky look on John's Facebook page showed me photos of Willis, a lean, very fit-looking eight-year-old thoroughbred. I guessed they would be the ones to beat.

Emilly was also in our race with Joe, using his official name, Another Chance III.

Rumours were rife that trained professional racehorses were taking part. One of our rivals, The Junior Man, sounded like one of them. I found the horse on the Racing Post website and discovered he had run in hurdle races at Wetherby earlier in the year and had previously raced against Neon Wolf, one of the leading fancies at that year's Cheltenham Festival. At six years old, The Junior Man was less than half Alexander's age.

"I don't think we'll be winning, but we'll give it our best shot," I said to Emilly. "I just want to finish in the first four, then we'll get into the Winner's Enclosure!"

It was 10am. I paced nervously around the yard, feeling physically sick. There were only three hours until the race.

I climbed into the wagon and, for the umpteenth time, checked inside my jockey bag, making sure I had not forgotten any of my attire. It was still all there.

I had breathed a huge sigh of relief when the horsebox's engine roared into life. It would have been a cruel, and not unpredictable, twist if it had chosen that morning not to start. Now the gleaming silver beast stood waiting for its precious cargo.

Alexander pranced around excitedly as Sue Dinsdale gave him a final brush and put on his travel boots and tail guard. Jenny had done much of the work the previous evening, brushing him, washing and conditioning his red tail and oiling his hooves. She had made a browband for his bridle from yellow and purple ribbon, to match our colours.

"He knows something is happening, but he doesn't know what," I said. "But I think he is old enough to cope when he gets to the racecourse."

While Alexander was excited, I felt sick with apprehension. The waiting was almost over, but until I could get on my horse I could not relax and start to enjoy the experience. The build up was just something to get through.

Jenny had spent nights lying awake in terror at the prospect of Alexander and I thundering down the racetrack. She feared I would lose my balance on the 'ridiculously flimsy' plastic saddle and be tossed under the pounding hooves of the other horses. She was working at the stables that morning but would be at the course in time for the race.

Finally, it was time to go. Alexander loaded easily, trotting eagerly into the back of the wagon. I secured the ramp door, jumped into the cab and turned on the engine.

"We're under starter's orders!" I said, and with a wave and a grin I towed Alexander down the drive.

After seven years, he was off to the races.

It is a fifteen minute journey to the racecourse. Now we were on our way, I felt calmer. I remembered us passing horseboxes heading to the races in years gone by, while we travelled to a showjumping event, and wondering if other people thought we were also going racing. This time we actually were.

I pulled off the main A59 road and trundled down a narrow country lane to the course. On our right I could see the massive steeplechase fences. Already there were cars parked up as spectators began to arrive.

I pulled into the field behind the parade ring, set aside for horseboxes and trailers, and switched off the engine. Alexander neighed loudly, announcing our arrival.

Ian and Karen were already there, relaxing in folding chairs and glancing at the race day programme. On page ten it listed the runners and riders for The Pendle Hunt Charity Challenge Flat Race. And there we were. Rider name – Steven Wright. Horse name – Adelphi Warrior.

We had been instructed to be at the track for 11am. The course walk was scheduled for 11.15am, with the safety and stewards' briefing half an hour after that.

Emilly arrived soon after and we set out to walk the course together. We said little as we tramped along, our heads bowed in contemplation as we examined the ground. It had recently been watered after a dry spell threatened to make the going too firm. Now it was perfect, with a covering of grass. I only found two very small divets all the way round.

The walk seemed to be over in a flash. Time seemed frozen.

I had already given Alexander's passport to the secretary at declaration, and handed over the charity sponsorship money. People had continued to be generous and I had raised more than £500, double the minimum target.

Now it was time for the briefing with the stewards. The charity riders formed a circle just inside the officials tent. Many of us looked pensive and laughed nervously as we absorbed our instructions, intended to make sure we came back in one piece. It seemed unreal, as if I was observing something happening to somebody else. But this was my moment.

Again we were warned not to attack the steep uphill gradient.

"If you do, you won't get round. Look after your horses and look after yourselves," said one of the stewards.

That was my intention. My main target was to bring us home safe. Anything else was a bonus.

With a final 'go out and enjoy yourselves' the briefing was over. I found myself back outside the tent, staring without seeing at the racetrack.

I checked the clock on my phone. There was less than an hour to go. It was time to collect my number and prepare to get on my racehorse.

Fighting for position in the race (pic by Alex Raistrick)

Chapter Twenty-Five

The Race

I took one final deep breath and stared down the racecourse, stretching away in front of us. I again patted Alexander on the neck, more to reassure me than him, and heard Ian's parting words: "Enjoy yourself," as he let go of the reins.

The instant he did so, Alexander launched himself forward into a brisk canter and took us down the course towards the start. In that moment, any lingering doubts I'd had about him wanting to race vanished.

Now we were on our own, our fate in front of us, and I was glad. Finally, I could enjoy it. For all the reassurance Ian had given me in the last few minutes, this was what I had spent the last two months working towards. Just me and Alexander alone on the racetrack, living our dream.

For it was not just my dream. Against all my expectations, Alexander was also living it. His ears were pricked as he took everything in, he shook his head from side to side with pure enthusiasm and I felt an electricity in his body that spoke of his pleasure at being able to run and compete on the track once more.

I pushed my heels down securely in the stirrups and raised my body out of the saddle as we headed up the track, away from the crowds. At last I could breathe more easily and relax. I could see other horses ahead and I knew there were a couple more following us. Officials and spectators lined the sides of the course as we cantered along, but I hardly noticed them. All that mattered now was Alexander and I, and the race we were about to run.

I squeezed him into a faster canter, recalling the advice of friends to let him have a blow on the way to the start so his airways would be clear and ready for the race. I peered between his ears, which flicked from side to side as we ran. Our momentum sent his orange mane flying in front of my face. We were heading up the gently sloping hill. I could see that other runners had reached the start and were now walking round. I asked Alexander to slow up and he responded by tossing his head from side to side in protest.

Ian's warning that Alexander would be strong when we cantered down to post had been justified. But he wasn't fighting me and he obediently dropped back to a walk, blowing a little as I had wanted him to.

"Good lad," I said, and stroked his neck reassuringly.

One of the starters strode up and checked the tightness of Alexander's girth. He was happy it was secure and patted him on the neck as he walked away.

Now we began to walk a circle behind the start. Alexander continued to throw his head around, yanking my arms time and again. The adrenaline was flowing through him. The other horses seemed settled, but mine was starting to kick up such a fuss the starter looked over at him with concern. But I felt calm, and my experiences over the last seven years now came to the fore. I drew on the lessons I had learned in those early traumatic years when Alexander was young and unpredictable and the memories of racing were still fresh in his head. I lengthened the reins and relaxed my hands and body. I stretched out my hand to stroke his neck and spoke quiet words of reassurance. He began to chill. He still tossed his head but he felt a little less tense and he walked forward more calmly.

Then one of the starters shouted: "Five minutes."

That was how long we still had before the race could begin. We had got down to the start early and would have to wait until the off time of 1.15, allowing punters to put on any late bets. I wondered fleetingly if we were still the favourites.

It was a long five minutes. We seemed to be in a time warp as we endlessly walked round and round. Alexander had grabbed hold of the bit and was now marching with his neck arched like a dressage horse. He kept twisting round to look eagerly down the track. He could barely contain himself. It seemed he could not wait to get going.

I had emptied my mind. I had no thought now about tactics. My focus was on Alexander and I felt at one with him.

Down by the winning post the crowds were gathered in anticipation, the sound of their chatter mixing with the sharp, clear tones of the race commentator.

But up at the start it was eerily quiet. We were unaware of the noise below. All we heard was the snorting of the horses.

A voice broke the silence: "You look the part, Steve!"

John Chadwick smiled as he rode past. He looked calm and confident. I shared his feelings. I was ready. The five minutes must surely be nearly over. I was suddenly aware of the starter standing on his rostrum, the white flag in his hand. Then I heard a voice calling us into line. Out of nowhere, the moment had arrived.

We were to the left of the other runners. I wanted Alexander to be on the outside, where I could keep him out of trouble and get him settled. We were in completely the wrong position.

The flag was now raised but I felt surprisingly calm. I knew the starter wouldn't set us off until we were all ready. I walked Alexander behind the rest of the field to the outside and turned him to face the front. Everyone was now standing in line. The start was imminent. The dream was about to happen.

We were a yard behind the others. I noticed that Emilly was on our immediate inside. Alexander began to walk forward.

"All right, off you go!" called the starter, and dropped the flag.

For a split second nothing happened, no one moved. Time seemed to stand still. And then Alexander curled his neck and body and propelled us forward with a great, powerful spring. The other horses set off in the same moment and the charge down the hill began.

I had considered riding Alexander from the front and try to grind down the opposition. But in the end I had decided that Plan A would be to hold him back, not far off the pace, and save his energy, then see what he had left towards the end of the race. But I knew the plan might have to change as the race unfolded.

My Plan A went instantly out of the window. Alexander had his own Plan A. He put his head down and galloped flat out. The horses to our left disappeared from view as we started to descend the hill. He was flying down it. A scary thought rushed through my brain, a reprise of Jenny's nightmare that I would plunge from the tiny saddle. But my balance had not deserted me. I felt secure as we pelted along.

The commentator announced: "Adelphi Warrior is very prominent at this stage. And indeed, Adelphi Warrior is the early leader as they gallop down the hill."

There was a cheer from Charles and the Farfield clan.

But I was not aware of the cheers, or the commentary. All I could hear was the wind in my ears and Alexander's hooves pounding on the turf.

My heart beat faster with the exhilaration of it. But my brain was still working clearly. Despite the thrill of the downhill gallop, I knew that I needed to get control of the partnership if my Plan A was going to work. I didn't want

Alexander to burn all his energy at the beginning. I yanked on the reins to bring him back, but he just tossed his head and kept on at the same speed.

"Come on, steady up lad," I shouted, pulling a second time at the reins. Again he threw his head to one side, but this time he listened and eased back to a three-quarter gallop.

Emilly and Joe came charging past on the inside, followed by another lady rider, but I was happy to settle into a close third. That was just where I wanted to be.

Then, as we reached the bottom of the hill, I noticed the big steeplechase fence looming up in the middle of the course on the run to the winning post. We were supposed to pass it on the inside. I still had Alexander on the outside. As we got nearer to the fence, I realised with alarm that our course was taking us towards the left edge of it. And Alexander had locked on to it.

"Bloody 'ell. He's setting us up to jump it!" I thought in horror.

Alexander's racing instinct had kicked in. He had been bred to jump steeplechase fences and here was one in his sights. There was only one thing for him to do. But it was not what I wanted!

"No, no, Man," I called out, instantly shoving him over to the left with my right leg. He responded immediately and we passed inside the fence with plenty of room to spare, and galloped past the winning post. One full circuit to go. About one mile.

We headed into the long sweeping left-hand bend in third place. I was happy tracking the two leaders. But the shape of the race suddenly changed. We were in the middle of the track. Emilly and the other horse were just ahead of us, when two other runners appeared from nowhere on our inside. I hadn't seen them coming. I wasn't aware of anything happening behind me. I glanced across to my left. The horse nearest to us was the racehorse, The Junior Man. It was being forced wider out by something else on its inside, which was obscured from my view. The Junior Man was edging closer to us.

"Alexander's not going to like this," I thought.

It was just the competitive situation I had feared. For the first time we were experiencing the hurly burly of a fight for racing position. The other two had the inside line and had got their noses in front. The only place for us to go was further out on the bend. I pushed Alexander across with my left leg. To my surprise he seemed unconcerned about the other horse edging towards him, and kept on galloping.

But we were being pushed wider and wider and as we emerged from the bend we had dropped back to fifth place, and a gap was opening up ahead.

"Adelphi Warrior has lost his position," the commentator announced.

I gave Alexander a squeeze, asking him to quicken up, and he cruised past the horse in front of us, into fourth place.

But everything was happening too quickly for me. I was struggling to keep up mentally. Ahead of us, The Junior Man, Emilly and Joe, and John Chadwick and Willis, were making a dash for it. I realised we were getting left behind. John had been the one making his move on the inside on the bend. He had pressed the accelerator hard and was now in the lead. I had thought about following John in the race. But I had been caught napping. I hadn't even seen him.

I squeezed Alexander again, asking for a little more, but I was reluctant to ask for too much. The big, steep hill was almost upon us and everyone had told me not to push him up it.

We were making ground on Emilly and Joe, and surged past them on the uphill climb. But the racing thoroughbreds were kicking for home and fighting their own battle. They were now ten to twenty lengths clear – it was hard for me to judge –

and were already disappearing around the bend at the crest of the hill.

Alexander was still going well, but he was blowing a bit, and I held true to my plan to give him a breather at the top. It was frustrating to see the two leaders going further clear as they raced away towards the downhill run to the finish. But I remembered the words of Sally Coates, and knew that we could not win. The most important thing was to look after my horse and bring him home safe. That had been my priority and it had not changed.

But we were still in third place and I was determined to finish there. At the top of the hill I asked Alexander to quicken again. He responded and for the second time we galloped down the hill. This time I didn't worry about falling off. We were not going flat out. There was no point pushing Alexander too hard. Third place was the best we were going to get. Now I felt relaxed, and for the first time I was able to forget the focus on race tactics and simply enjoy the experience; the unbelievable feeling of riding Alexander in a race.

And I was riding him into a place. I looked behind me as we hit the bottom of the hill and faced up to the final 200 yards to the line, and could not see another runner anywhere near us.

"We've nearly done it, Man!" I shouted.

The winning post was coming up. Alexander's ears were pricked and he was tossing his head again, wanting to go faster, but I eased him back to a canter as we crossed the line.

We had done it! We had run our race and we had finished third. I struggled to take it in. Not only was I living my dream but I felt in a dream-like state, as if I was inside a protective bubble which made everything else outside it – the crowds, the other runners, the course – seem ghostly and unreal.

Then reality kicked in and I remembered Keith Rosier's warning words. I checked carefully behind me for other horses that could run into the back of us, before pulling Alexander up. There were none. We were well clear of the rest of the field.

It had taken us just under three and a half minutes to complete the course and it had passed in a blur. I hadn't had time to be scared, or to savour the thrill of it all. But a thrill it had certainly been.

People were lined three deep to clap and cheer us as we walked from the course and back down the walkway. Somewhere in the crowd a man's voice called out: "Well done, Steve." I could not pinpoint who the voice belonged to or where it came from. I was in a complete daze. My ambition had been achieved, but it was washing over me.

I was suddenly aware of Sue and Ian. Sue had hold of the reins and was leading Alexander into the place I had hoped to get into – the Winner's Enclosure – while Ian walked beside us.

I found myself rabbiting about how Alexander had burned up too much energy at the start.

"You got really taken out on the bend," Sue added.

And then we were in the Winner's Enclosure and standing in the designated spot for third place. People were still cheering and waving. At the front were Jenny and Sophie, their faces lit up with delight. I beamed back. It was so important they were there to share my joy.

I stayed in the saddle for a few more seconds, milking every moment. Finally, I dismounted and put my arms around Alexander's neck. I grinned at my family and friends and announced: "That was brilliant!"

When the saddle was removed I could see Alexander was lathered in sweat, and Ian threw buckets of water over him to cool him. But Alexander's ears were up, his eyes were bright and he too seemed to be making the most of it. As he stood there, his neck and sides wet with the sweat of effort and excitement, he seemed to know he had done well. He stared around him, eyeing the crowd with a look that was almost defiant, as if to say: "Now you know what I can do." And he had succeeded. I flung my arm around his neck and hugged him again until it was time to leave the arena and head back to the wagon.

I watched my horse as Sue walked him round the field. He still seemed full of energy and enthusiasm and every time the commentator's voice boomed out Alexander stopped, stood tall and proud and gazed back towards the course. It seemed that he wanted another go.

I sat on the wagon steps and collected my thoughts. It had been over so quickly and I also wanted another go. I had thought the race would be a one-off for us. Now I wasn't so sure.

One thing I was certain about – my pride in Alexander. We had enjoyed so much success at showjumping, cross-country and one-day eventing. But for the first time in his life as a racehorse he had got into the Winner's Enclosure. He deserved that.

It was days before the reality of what we had achieved sank in. Then I found myself assessing our performance.

I accepted that we could never have beaten the two racing thoroughbreds, which had been in full training and were half Alexander's age.

I knew I had been caught out on the bend, when John Chadwick, who narrowly won the race in a duelling finish, made his move. I had been tactically naive, but it was my first race and it had all happened so fast. Someone said we lost fifty yards on the bend, and it certainly set us back, but I had to be proud of our third place.

At the end of the race I felt Alexander had more left to give. Photos of him finishing, with his ears up and forward and his eyes bright, confirmed that. I could have asked him for more, but it wouldn't have got us a higher place so there was no point. I had no way of knowing what he would have in the petrol tank until we had done the race. I would know better next time – if there was a next time. But Alexander had found it so easy there was no reason why we shouldn't give it another go next year – if we were both fit and well.

"It's a shame there isn't another charity race in a couple of weeks time," Ian Conroy said. "He's fit enough."

Indeed he was. But if we never raced again, it wouldn't matter. We had done it now and we had shared the joy of it together.

Ian put it into perspective, and his words touched me.

He said: "I'm proud that you led the race and proud that you finished third. But I'm most proud of how you looked after each other. It was obvious what a strong partnership you have."

Keith's partner, Nicola, agreed. "Those two could go out and do anything together," she said.

I was moved by the kind words of well-wishers after the race. Charles texted: "You've done us proud!" while Ian sent a Facebook message: "I felt privileged to lead you and Herman on to the track. You did a great job on the donkey and looked after him. A massive well done!"

The support of hundreds of total strangers on a Facebook group was particularly humbling. The morning after the race, Jenny put a short message about us on the Racehorses, Where Are They Now site, with photos of us in action. She did it merely to give me a nice surprise, but the response was overwhelming. Within an hour and a half, it had 160 likes and a number of lovely comments. The entry ended up with more than 530 likes and loves - more than superstar racer Sprinter Sacre got when moving to his new home - and around 50 comments. They ranged from 'beautiful chestnut boy' and 'well done from all who live in Broadchurch' to 'I'm proud and I don't even know you' and 'living your dreams is what it's all about.'

I have lived my dream and I will never forget the thrill of it, but what gave me the most pleasure was how much Alexander loved racing again. He had been as thrilled as anyone.

And, after seven years, he has set the record straight. He has proved he can do it. The older, assured horse he now is has succeeded where the immature, uncertain one failed. Adelphi Warrior's race record now reads Last, Pulled Up, Third. I am so proud of him.

Our roller coaster journey together has spanned seven years. Our path has taken us from failure and unhappiness to the fulfillment of a dream.

But the dream is not over. While I have Alexander – my best friend and the four-legged partner I love – the dream will go on.

Crossing the finish line (pic by Lesley Tate)

37644135R00151

Printed in Great Britain
by Amazon